Academic Writing

Most international students need to write essays and reports for exams and coursework. Yet writing good academic English is one of the most demanding tasks students face. This new edition of *Academic Writing* has been fully revised to help students reach this goal. Clearly organised, the course explains the writing process from start to finish. Each stage is demonstrated and practised, from selecting suitable sources, reading, note-making and planning through to re-writing and proof-reading.

The four main parts of *Academic Writing* allow teachers and students to easily find the help they need. Each part is divided into short sections, which contain examples, explanations and exercises, for use in the classroom or self-study. Cross-references allow easy access to relevant sections, and a full answer key is featured on the companion website.

The third edition of this popular course builds on the success of the earlier editions and responds to suggestions from both students and teachers. Plagiarism has become a major concern in higher education, and a special feature of *Academic Writing* is a section on avoiding plagiarism. There are also units on the key skills of paraphrasing, summarising and referencing.

The book includes sections on crucial areas such as argument, cause and effect, comparison, definitions and academic style. Working in groups, dealing with graphs, charts and numbers and giving examples are explained in detail. Another part deals with accuracy in writing, providing practice with topics such as vocabulary, conjunctions and prepositions. The final part provides a range of writing models of both short and longer essays and reports. A new companion website offers further practice with a range of additional exercises, including answers.

All international students wanting to maximise their academic potential will find this practical and easy-to-use book a valuable guide to writing in English for their degree courses.

Stephen Bailey is a freelance teacher and writer of materials for English for Academic Purposes. He has taught international students for many years at the University of Nottingham, UK, and has previously worked in the Czech Republic, Japan, Malaysia and Spain.

International students have many adjustments to make as they enter British universities and Stephen's book makes at least one area of their lives – academic study – much more approachable. With its straightforward approach and improved layout, it will be a book many students will come to regard as an essential companion to their university lives.

Stephen Dewhirst, *Freelance EAP teacher, UK*

Stephen Bailey has produced an excellent new edition of his popular book Academic Writing. This book presents a great blend of advice and practice. The advice focuses on what is required in terms of academic writing at university. He addresses different types of academic writing and even includes sample writing texts. The practice breaks down academic writing by focussing on the language typically required in academic settings with lots of student exercises. His book takes the international student writer through the process of academic writing, moving from understanding academic writing tasks to using reading sources through to revising and drafting the final text.

Dr Lindy Woodrow, *Director China Education Centre,*
University of Sydney, Australia

International students and indeed all students should find this book very helpful. It is accessible to read and engages in an explicit and sharply focused manner with many elements of the critical use of reading, of writing and of studying. The book usefully explains, exemplifies, and tests understanding. It deals with the problematic areas of plagiarism and grammatical work, of developing argument and counter argument, and essay expression. It should be very useful for international students engaged in academic writing.

Professor Gina Wisker, *University of Brighton, UK*

Stephen Bailey's Academic Writing is one of the few academic writing books that deal with core areas effectively - language, text type, academic conventions and the writing process. This is done by giving simple explanations, authentic examples and useful practice opportunities which can either be done in class or as self study. The book appeals to a range of levels including pre and in sessional students and equips them with a range of the key language and skills needed to embark on academic writing in higher education.

Fiona Gilbert, *Oxford Brookes University, UK*

The third edition of *Academic Writing: A Handbook for International Students* will be welcome by all students new to academic writing in English-medium colleges and universities. The book is carefully set out to guide students step by step through the maze of assignment types, writing conventions and mysterious vocabulary they will find when entering higher education. Moving from the writing process through common patterns of grammar and argument to models of literature reviews, essays and reports, the handbook offers a clear, practical and accessible introduction to the skills students will need to write effectively at university.

Professor Ken Hyland, *University of Hong Kong*

This book provides international students with a useful introduction to the basic practices in reading and writing for academic purposes. It includes topics such as the typical content of article abstracts, the mechanics of citation and referencing, and some uses of sources in writing – topics that will help international students, studying in an English medium university for the first time, to meet their tutors' expectations in reading and writing assignments. The chapter on reading advises a critical attitude to internet resources, advice most relevant to students today.

Antonia Chandrasegaran, *National Institute of Education, Singapore*

Academic Writing

A Handbook for International Students

Third edition

Stephen Bailey

Routledge
Taylor & Francis Group

LONDON AND NEW YORK

First edition published 2003
by Routledge

Second edition published 2006
by Routledge

This edition published 2011
by Routledge
2 Park Square, Milton Park, Abingdon, Oxon OX14 4RN

Simultaneously published in the USA and Canada
by Routledge
270 Madison Avenue, New York, NY 10016

Routledge is an imprint of the Taylor & Francis Group, an informa business

© 2011 Stephen Bailey

Typeset in Galliard by
Florence Production Ltd, Stoodleigh, Devon
Printed and bound in Great Britain by
Ashford Colour Press Ltd

British Library Cataloguing in Publication Data
A catalogue record for this book is available from the British Library

Library of Congress Cataloging-in-Publication Data
Bailey, Stephen, 1947–
    Academic writing for international studies of business/
    Stephen Bailey. – 1st ed.
        p. cm.
        Includes bibliographical references and index.
    1. Authorship.   2. Academic writing.   3. Business writing.
    I. Title.
    PN151.B26 2011
    808′.06665 – dc22   2010014023

ISBN13: 978–0–415–59580–3 (hbk)
ISBN13: 978–0–415–59581–0 (pbk)
ISBN13: 978–0–203–83165–6 (ebk)

Contents

Acknowledgements

I would like to thank the many staff and students at the Centre for English Language Education (CELE) at the University of Nottingham who have helped develop these materials over a number of years. In particular I should mention Steve Dewhirst, John Hall, Sandra Haywood, Mick Kavanagh, Ann Kavanagh, Richard Lee, John Rabone and Ann Smith, who have helped me unravel some of the finer points of academic language.

My wife Rene has again provided me with invaluable support, encouragement and advice on many aspects of academic writing during the development of this project. Final thanks are due to my daughter, Sophie, for helping me keep the whole subject in perspective!

Introduction for teachers

This course has been developed to help international students with their written assignments in English at both undergraduate and postgraduate level. Students who are not native speakers of English often find the written demands of their courses very challenging. In addition to the vocabulary of academic English they have to learn new conventions of style, referencing and format. Furthermore, their lecturers are often concerned by their lack of critical thinking skills, and also mention students' failure to answer the specific question and their inability to develop answers logically. Issues around vocabulary, plagiarism and referencing skills are significant additional worries.

Academic Writing: A Handbook for International Students sets out to address these problems directly. It recognises that while international students are not expected to write perfect English, accurate and effective language use is an essential skill for such students. What may be individually minor problems with prepositions, word endings, spelling or articles can result in essays that are barely comprehensible to the best-motivated marker.

To deal with this students are guided through the stages of the writing process in Part 1 and then the related writing skills are explained and practised in Part 2. Part 3 is designed as a reference guide to tackle the main problems of accuracy, while Part 4 provides examples of some common formats. Teachers may wish to work through the writing process in Part 1 while referring to units in Part 2 as the group progresses. (Part 2 is not intended to be taught from start to finish: note the alphabetical organisation of Parts 2 and 3.)

A feature of *Academic Writing* is its clear and logical organisation, which makes it ideal as a self-study and reference guide for students needing to work independently. This is a recognition that most courses in academic writing are inevitably time-constrained, and that some students may have no other option. It is designed to be used on both pre-sessional and in-sessional courses, and is suitable for subject-specific (e.g. law, medicine) and multi-discipline courses in English for Academic Purposes (EAP).

Part	Topic	Main Application
1	**The writing process** from finding sources to proof-reading	Classroom use
2	**Elements of writing** from argument to working in groups	Classroom use and self-study
3	**Accuracy in writing** from abbreviations to verb tenses	Classroom use, self-study and reference
4	**Writing models** from letters to longer essays	Self-study and reference

Academic Writing uses authentic texts and examples taken from a wide range of disciplines. Extensive cross-referencing is provided to assist both teacher and students in finding relevant support. All exercises can be done individually or in pairs and groups. A full range of answers plus some extra practice exercises are available on the book's website: (http://cw.routledge.com/textbooks/bailey) or email: education@routledge.com

The material in this course has been extensively tested in the classroom, but improvements can always be achieved. Therefore I would be very glad to receive any comments or suggestions about the book from teachers or students for future editions.

Stephen Bailey

Introduction for students

What is the purpose of the book?

This book is designed to help you succeed in the writing tasks you may be given as part of your academic course. The kind of writing that you are asked to do may be different from the assignments you have done before, and for some this may be the first time you have had to write long essays or reports in English.

Your teachers know that English is not your native language and will be sympathetic to the problems you have in your writing. But at the same time you will want to learn to write as clearly and accurately as possible, not only to succeed on your current course but also in preparation for your career. Almost all large companies and organisations expect their staff to be able to communicate effectively in written English, as well as orally. Therefore, during your studies you have the ideal opportunity to learn to write English well, and this book can help you achieve that goal.

In addition to accuracy, students on academic courses are expected to take a critical approach to their sources. This means that your teachers will expect you to question and evaluate everything you read, asking whether it is reliable or relevant. You are also expected to refer carefully to the sources of all your ideas, using a standard system of referencing. *Academic Writing: A Handbook for International Students* will help you to develop these skills.

Managing your time

Many teachers complain about work that is handed in late or shows signs of having been finished in a hurry. This leads to poor marks, and can be avoided by better time management. This means planning your time carefully from the start of the course so that your work is never late or rushed.

■ **Decide if the following ideas about time management are true or false:**

(a) Essay deadlines are often several months after the course starts.   (T/F)

(b) The best way to plan an assignment is to use some kind of wall chart.   (T/F)

(c) Reading and note-making often take longer than writing.   (T/F)

(d) The best time to study is after midnight.   (T/F)

(e) It's a good idea to make time every day to relax with friends.   (T/F)

In fact, all of these are true except for (d): it's better to study during the day and then get a good night's sleep. The key point is to schedule the work for each task week by week, so that you allocate time for drafting, re-writing and proof-reading. By doing this you will avoid the last-minute panic that leads to poor marks and having to re-take courses.

Using the book

The book can be used either with a teacher or for self-study and reference. Each unit contains practice exercises that can be checked using the answer key on the website. For ease of use it is divided into the following sections:

Part 1 The writing process

This follows the process of writing from the reading stage through to proof-reading.

Part 2 Elements of writing

The key writing skills, organised alphabetically from argument to working in groups.

Part 3 Accuracy in writing

This section revises and practises areas of grammar and vocabulary, again arranged alphabetically, from abbreviations to verb tenses.

Part 4 Writing models

Gives examples of letters and emails, CVs, reports, case studies and longer essays.

To help you get the most out of this course, note the following points:

- Instructions are printed in a display type, for example:

  ■ **List your ideas below**

- Links to relevant units are shown like this:

  ▶ **See Unit 4.5 Writing longer essays**

  These links help you to find extra information, but do not have to be read in order to complete the exercises.

- Extra practice in some areas is provided on the *Academic Writing* website (http://cw.routledge.com/textbooks/bailey). This is shown by:

  @ Referencing>

- Answers are provided for most exercises on the website. If no definite answer can be given, an example answer is usually offered.

- The **index** can be used to locate specific information. The **glossary** explains academic terms that you may not be familiar with.

- *WARNING!*
  Every semester many students lose vital written work because of lost or broken laptops. Make a habit of backing up your files onto a memory stick at least once a day.

Thousands of students have already found that *Academic Writing* helps them to write more clearly and effectively. This new edition has been developed using their feedback and ideas, and I would be very glad to receive comments and suggestions on any aspect of the book to help develop further editions.

Stephen Bailey

Academic writing quiz

■ **How much do you know about academic writing?**
Find out by doing this fun quiz.

1   The main difference between academic writing and normal
    writing is that academic writing:

    (a) uses longer words

    (b) tries to be precise and unbiased

    (c) is harder to understand

2   The difference between a project and an essay is:

    (a) essays are longer

    (b) projects are longer

    (c) students choose projects' topics

3   Teachers complain most about students:

    (a) not answering the question given

    (b) not writing enough

    (c)   not referencing properly

4   The best time to write an introduction is often:

    (a) first

    (b) last

    (c) after writing the main body

5   Plagiarism is:

    (a) a dangerous disease

    (b) an academic offence

    (c) an academic website

6   Making careful notes is essential for:

   (a) writing essays

   (b) revising for exams

   (c) all academic work

7   An in-text citation looks like:

   (a) (Manton, 2008)

   (b) (Richard Manton, 2008)

   (c) (Manton, R. 2008)

8   Paraphrasing a text means:

   (a) making it shorter

   (b) changing a lot of the vocabulary

   (c) adding more detail

9   Paragraphs always contain:

   (a) six or more sentences

   (b) an example

   (c) a topic sentence

10 The purpose of an introduction is:

   (a) to give your aims and methods

   (b) to excite the reader

   (c) to summarise your ideas

11 Proof-reading means:

   (a) getting a friend to check your work

   (b) checking for minor errors

   (c) re-writing

12 Teachers expect students to adopt a critical approach to their sources:

   (a) sometimes

   (b) only for Master's work

   (c) always

The writing process

Background to writing

Most academic courses assess students through written assignments. These include coursework, which may take weeks to write, and exam answers, which often have to be written in an hour or less. This unit deals with:

- The names of different writing tasks
- The format of long and short writing tasks
- The use of sentences and paragraphs

1 The purpose of academic writing

Writers should be clear why they are writing. The most common reasons for writing include:

- to report on a piece of research the writer has conducted
- to answer a question the writer has been given or chosen
- to discuss a subject of common interest and give the writer's view
- to synthesise research done by others on a topic

■ **Can you suggest any other reasons?**

-

In all cases it is useful to bear in mind the likely readers of your work. How can you explain your ideas to them effectively? Although there is no fixed standard of academic writing, it is clearly different from the written style of newspapers or novels. Similarly, it is generally agreed that academic writing attempts to be accurate and objective. What are its other features?

■ **Working alone or in a group, list your ideas below.**

- *Impersonal style* _____

- _____

- _____

- _____

2 Common types of academic writing

Below are the most common types of written work produced by students.

■ **Match the terms on the left to the definitions on the right.**

Notes	A piece of research, either individual or group work, with the topic chosen by the student(s).
Report	The longest piece of writing normally done by a student (20,000+ words) often for a higher degree, on a topic chosen by the student.
Project	A written record of the main points of a text or lecture, for a student's personal use.
Essay	A general term for any academic essay, report, presentation or article.
Dissertation/ Thesis	A description of something a student has done e.g. conducting a survey.
Paper	The most common type of written work, with the title given by the teacher, normally 1000–5000 words.

3 The format of long and short writing tasks

Short essays (including exam answers) generally have this pattern:

Introduction

Main body

Conclusion

Longer essays may include:

Introduction

Main body
  Literature review
  Case study
  Discussion

Conclusion
References
Appendices

▶ **See Units 4.3 Reports, case studies and literature reviews and 4.5 Writing longer essays**

Dissertations and journal articles may have:

Abstract
List of contents
List of tables
Introduction

Main body
  Literature review
  Case study
  Findings
  Discussion

Conclusion
Acknowledgements
References
Appendices

■ **Find the words in the lists above that match the following definitions:**

(a) A short summary of 100–200 words, which explains the paper's purpose and main findings.

_____

(b) A list of all the sources the writer has mentioned in the text.

_____

(c) A section, at the end, where additional information is included.

_____

(d) A short section where people who have helped the writer are thanked.

_____

(e) Part of the main body in which the writer discusses relevant research.

_____

(f) A section where one particular example is described in detail.

_____

4 The features of academic writing

There is considerable variation in the format of academic writing required by different schools and departments. Your teachers may give you guidelines, or you should ask them what they want. But some general features apply to most formats.

■ **Read the text below and identify the features underlined, using the words in the box.**

sentence	heading	sub-title
paragraph	title	phrase

(a) **A fishy story**

(b) Misleading health claims regarding omega-3 fatty acids

(c) Introduction

(d) <u>There has been considerable discussion recently about the benefits of omega-3 fatty acids in the diet.</u> (e) <u>It is claimed that</u> these reduce the risk of cardiovascular disease and may even combat obesity. Consequently food producers have added omega-3s to products ranging from margarine to soft drinks in an attempt to make their products appear healthier and hence increase sales.

(f) <u>However, consumers may be unaware that there are two types of omega-3s. The best (long-chain fatty acids) are derived from fish, but others (short-chain fatty acids) come from cheaper sources such as soya. This latter group have not been shown to produce the health benefits linked to the long-chain variety. According to Tamura *et al.* (2009) positive results may only be obtained either by eating oily fish three times a week, or by taking daily supplements containing 500mg of eicosapentaenoic acid (EPA) or docosahexaenoic acid (DHA).</u>

(a) _____

(b) _____

(c) _____

(d) _____

(e) _____

(f) _____

5 Some other common text features

(a) **Reference** to sources using **citation**:
According to Tamura et al. (2009)

(b) The use of **abbreviations** to save space:
docosahexaenoic acid (DHA)

(c) **Italics:** used to show words from other languages:
Tamura *et al.* (= and others)

(d) **Brackets:** used to give subsidiary information or to clarify a point:
. . . but others (short-chain fatty acids) come from cheaper sources such as soya.

6 Simple and complex sentences

■ Study the table below.

Annual vehicle production 2005–9

2005	2006	2007	2008	2009
135,470	156,935	164,820	159,550	123,075

All sentences contain verbs:

> In 2005 the company **produced** over 135,000 vehicles.
>
> Between 2005 and 2006 vehicle production **increased** by 20 per cent.

Simple sentences are easier to write and read, but complex sentences are also needed in academic writing. However, students should make clarity a priority, and avoid writing very complex sentences until they feel confident in their ability.Complex sentences contain **conjunctions, relative pronouns** or **punctuation,** which link the clauses:

> In 2005 the company produced over 135,000 vehicles **but** between 2005 and 2006 production increased by 20 per cent.
>
> Over 164,000 vehicles were produced in 2007; by 2009 this had fallen to 123,000.

■ Write two simple and two complex sentences using data from the table above.

(a) _____

_____

(b) _____

_____

(c) _____

_____

(d) _____

_____

7 Writing in paragraphs

■ **Discuss the following questions:**

What is a paragraph?

Why are texts divided into paragraphs?

How long are paragraphs?

Do paragraphs have a standard structure?

■ **Read the text below and divide it into a suitable number of paragraphs.**

7.1 BIOCHAR

Charcoal is produced by burning wood slowly in a low-oxygen environment. This material, which is mainly carbon, was used for many years to heat iron ore to extract the metal. But when Abraham Darby discovered a smelting process using coke (produced from coal) in 1709 demand for charcoal collapsed. At approximately the same time the carbon dioxide level in the atmosphere began to rise. But a new use for charcoal, re-named biochar, has recently emerged. It is claimed that using biochar made from various types of plants can both improve soil quality and combat global warming. Various experiments in the United States have shown that adding burnt crop wastes to soil increases fertility and cuts the loss of vital nutrients such as nitrates. The other benefit of biochar is its ability to lock CO_2 into the soil. The process of decay normally allows the carbon dioxide in plants to return to the atmosphere rapidly, but when transformed into charcoal this may be delayed for hundreds of years. In addition, soil containing biochar appears to release less methane, a gas which contributes significantly to global warming. American researchers claim that widespread use of biochar could reduce global CO_2 emissions by over 10 per cent. But other agricultural scientists are concerned about the environmental effects of growing crops especially for burning, and about the displacement of food crops that might be caused. However, the potential twin benefits of greater farm yields and reduced greenhouse gases mean that further research in this area is urgently needed.

▶ See Unit 1.10 Organising paragraphs

Examples of types of academic texts

Argument and discussion	Unit 2.1 and Website
Case studies	Unit 4.3
Cause and effect	Unit 2.2
Classification	Website
Comparisons	Unit 2.4 and Website
Descriptions	Website
Laboratory reports	Website
Literature reviews	Unit 4.3
Problems and solutions	Unit 2.9
Recommendations	Website
Reports	Unit 4.3
Survey reports	Unit 4.4

Reading: finding suitable sources

Students often underestimate the importance of effective reading, but on any course it is vital to be able to locate the most relevant and suitable sources. This unit:

- examines the most appropriate text types for academic work
- explores ways of locating relevant material in the library
- explains the use of electronic resources

1 Academic texts

You need to read a variety of text types for your course, so it is important to identify suitable types and recognise their features. This will help you to assess their value.

■ **You are studying Tourism Marketing. Read the text extracts 1–4 below and decide which are the most suitable for academic use, and why.**

Text	Suitability?
1	*Yes, it summarises some relevant research, and includes citations*
2	
3	
4	

1.1 To promote tourism and market destination, it is important to study the tourists' attitude, behaviour and demand. The studies of Levitt (1986) and Kotler and Armstrong (1994) suggest that an understanding of consumer behaviour may help with the marketing planning process in tourism marketing. The research of consumer behaviour is the key to the underpinning of all marketing activity, which is carried out to develop, promote and sell tourism products (Swarbrooke and Horner, 1999; Asad, 2005). Therefore, the study of consumer behaviour has become necessary for the sake of tourism marketing.

1.2 The romance of travel has always fascinated me, and our recent trip to Thailand lived up to expectations. We flew from Dubai and after a comfortable flight arrived in Bangkok just as the sun was rising. Our stay in the city lasted only a couple of days before we set off for the hill country around Chang Mai, where we were planning to visit some of the indigenous tribes who live in this mountainous region. When we arrived the weather was rather disappointing, but after a day the heavy rain gave way to sparkling clear sunshine.

1.3 Holiday trips to the Antarctica have quadrupled in the past decade and last year more than 46,000 people visited the land mass and surrounding oceans. However, safety fears and concerns about the impact visitors are having on the delicate frozen landscape have soared and members of the Antarctic Treaty – an agreement between 28 nations, including the UK, on the use of the continent – are now meeting to discuss ways to regulate tourism.

British officials are seeking to establish a 'strategic agreement for tourism' around the South Pole. If successful, it will see treaty members introduce new measures to improve the safety of tourist trips, while also reducing the impact that visitors will have on the environment. The regulations could see limits on the number of ships and landings, restrictions on how close they come to shore, a ban on building tourist facilities and hotels on the continent, and rules on waste discharges from ships.

1.4   Equally, from a political perspective, the nature of state involvement in and policies for tourism is dependent on both the political-economic structures and the prevailing political ideology in the destination state, with comparisons typically made between market-led and centrally planned economies. For example, the Thatcher–Reagan-inspired neo-liberalism of the 1980s, and the subsequent focus on privatisation and the markets in many Western nations contrasted starkly with the then centrally planned tourism sectors in the former Eastern Europe (Buckley and Witt, 1990; Hall, 1991). At the same time, of course, it has also long been recognised that the political-economic relationship of one nation with another or with the wider international community (that is, the extent of political-economic dependency) may represent a significant influence on tourism development (Telfer, 2002). Thus, in short, tourism planning and development in the destination tends to reflect both the structures and political ideologies of the state and its international political-economic relations.

■ **The main features of academic texts are listed in the table below. Find examples of each using the texts above.**

Feature	Examples
1 Formal vocabulary	*the marketing planning process in tourism marketing . . . the extent of political-economic dependency . . .*
2 Use of references	
3 Impersonal style	
4 Long, complex sentences	

2 Types of text

■ The table below lists the most common written sources used by students. Work with a partner to consider their likely advantages and disadvantages.

Text type	Advantages	Disadvantages
Textbook	*Written for students*	*May be too general*
Website		
Journal article		
Official report (e.g. from government)		
Newspaper or magazine article		
e-book		

3 Using reading lists

Your teacher may give you a printed reading list, or it may be available online through the library website. The list will usually include textbooks, journal articles and websites. If the list is electronic there will be links to the library catalogue to let you check on the availability of the material. If the list is printed, you will have to use the library catalogue to find the texts. You do not have to read every word of a book because it is on the list. Your teacher will probably suggest which pages to read, and also tell you which parts are the most important. On reading lists you will find the following formats:

Books
   Miles, T. R. *Dyslexia: A Hundred Years On* / T.R. Miles and
   Elaine Miles, 2nd ed. Open University Press, 1999.

Journal articles
   Paulesu E. *et al.* Dyslexia: Cultural Diversity and Biological
   Unity. *Science*, 2001, 291, pages 2165–7.

Websites
   www.well.ox.ac.uk/monaco/dyslexia.shtml

4 Using library catalogues

University and college libraries usually have online catalogues. These allow
students to search for the materials they want in various ways. If the title
and author's name are known it is easy to check if the book is available,
but if you are making a search for material on a specific topic you may
have to vary the search terms. For instance, if you have been given an essay
title:

   'Is there a practical limit on the height of tall buildings?
   Illustrate your answer with reference to some recent
   skyscrapers.'

you might try:

   Skyscraper design

   Skyscraper construction

   Design of tall building

   Construction of tall buildings

If you use a very specific phrase you will probably only find a few titles.
'Skyscraper construction', for example, only produced three items in one
library database, but a more general term such as 'skyscrapers' found 57.

■   **You have entered the term 'skyscrapers' in the library catalogue
    search engine, and these are the first eight results. In order to
    answer the essay title above, which would you select to borrow?
    Give your reasons.**

Full details	Title	Ed/ Year	Location	Holdings
1	Skyscraper: the politics and power of building New York city in the twentieth century / Benjamin Flowers.	c2009	Main library	Availability
2	Skyscraper for the XXI century / edited by Carlo Aiello.	2008	Science library	Availability
3	Taipei 101 / Georges Binder [editor].	2008	Main library	Availability
4	Tall buildings: image of the skyscraper / Scott Johnson.	2008	Fine Arts Library	Availability
5	Skyscrapers: Fabulous Buildings that Reach for the Sky / Herbert Wright.	2008	Main library	Availability
6	Eco skyscrapers / Ken Yeang.	3rd Ed. 2007	Science library	Availability
7	Cost optimization of structures: fuzzy logic, genetic algorithms, and parallel computing / Hojjat Adeli, Kamal C. Sarma.	2006	Science library	Availability
8	Skyscrapers: a social history of the very tall building in America / by George H. Douglas.	2004	Main library	Availability

Full details
If you click on this you will get more information about the book, including the number of pages and a summary of the contents. This may help you decide whether to borrow it.

Ed/year
If a book has had more than one edition it suggests that it is a successful title.
The books are listed by the most recent first; always try to use the most up-to-date sources.

Location
Many large universities have more than one library. This tells you which one the book is kept in.

Holdings
If you click on availability it will tell you how many copies the library holds and if they are available to borrow or out on loan.

5 Using library websites to search electronic resources

E-journals and other electronic resources such as subject databases are becoming increasingly important. Their advantage is that they can be accessed by computer, saving the need to visit the library and find a text. Most library websites have a separate portal or gateway for searching electronic resources. This allows you to enter the name of a specific journal, or look for possible journals in your subject area by entering a term such as 'international business law'. In this case, the database may offer the following titles:

European Business Law Review

European Business Organisation Law Review

International Trade and Business Law Review

Law and Business Review of the Americas

In each case, you can access a list of issues available, which will let you read a list of published articles. Most journals publish four issues per year. In the case of *European Business Organisation Law Review*, the list would include:

Dec 2009 Vol. 10 Issue 4

Sep 2009 Vol. 10 Issue 3

June 2009 Vol. 10 Issue 2

Mar 2009 Vol. 10 Issue 1

By clicking on any of these issues you can read a full list of articles. It is usually sufficient to read the abstract to find out if the article will be relevant to your work. Note that most journal websites contain a search engine to allow you to search all back issues by subject. They may also offer links to articles in other journals on the same topic.

The best way to become familiar with these methods is to practise. Library websites usually contain tutorials for new students, and librarians are always willing to give help and advice when needed.

■ **Select a specific topic from your subject area.**

(a) Use the library catalogue to search for relevant books. Write down the most useful titles.

(b) Look for a few relevant journal articles, using the library portal. Write a reference for each article.

Reading: developing critical approaches

Students are expected to adopt a critical approach to sources, which requires a full understanding of written texts. This unit

- explains effective reading methods
- examines common text features, including abstracts
- explores and practises a critical analysis of texts

1 Reading methods

It is easy for students to underestimate the importance of reading skills. Especially for international students, reading academic texts in the quantity required for most courses is a demanding task. But students will not benefit from attending lectures and seminars unless the reading is done promptly, while clearly most writing tasks require extensive reading.

Moreover, the texts often contain new vocabulary and phrases, and may be written in a rather formal style. This means that distinct methods have to be adopted to cope with the volume of reading required, which is especially important when you are reading in another language. Clearly, you do not have time to read every word published on the topic you are studying. The chart below illustrates an approach to finding and dealing with texts.

■ **Complete the empty boxes in the chart with the following techniques:**

- Read intensively to make notes on key points
- Scan text for information you need (e.g. names)
- Survey text features (e.g. abstract, contents, index)

Choosing suitable texts

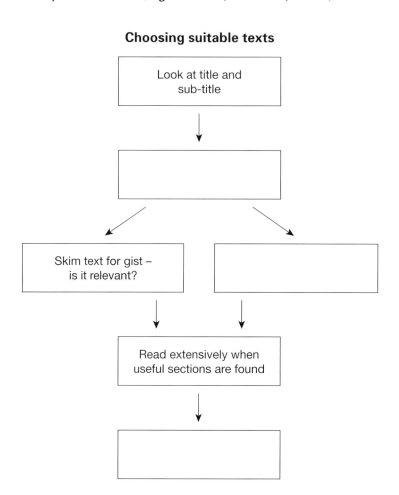

■ **Can you suggest any other reading skills to add to the chart above?**

2 Titles, sub-titles and text features

Many books and articles have both a title and a sub-title:

> The Right to Have Rights: Citizenship Practice and the
> Political Constitution of the EU.

The title is usually shorter; the sub-title often gives more information
about the focus.

After finding a relevant text, it is worth checking the following text features
before starting to read:

Author
Is the writer well-known in his/ her field? What else has he/ she
published?

Publication date and edition
Do not use a first edition if there is a (revised) second edition
available.

Abstract
See section below.

Contents
A list of the main chapters or sections. This should tell you what
proportion of the text is devoted to the topic you are researching.

Introduction or preface
This is where the author often explains his/ her reasons for
writing, and also how the text is organised.

References
This list shows all the sources used by the author and referred to
in the text. It should give you some suggestions for further
reading.

Bibliography
These are the sources the author has used but not specifically
referred to.

Index
An alphabetical list of all the topics and names mentioned in a
book. If, for example, you are looking for information about a
person, the index will tell you if that person is mentioned, and
how often.

3 Reading abstracts

They are normally found in peer-reviewed journal articles, where they act as a kind of summary to enable researchers to decide if it is worth reading the full article. As a student you will not normally have to write abstracts, but it is important to be able to read them effectively.

■ **Study this example:**

3.1 **CITIZENSHIP NORMS AND THE EXPANSION OF POLITICAL PARTICIPATION**

Russell J. Dalton

A growing chorus of scholars laments the decline of political participation in America, and the negative implications of this trend for American democracy. This article questions this position – arguing that previous studies misdiagnosed the sources of political change and the consequences of changing norms of citizenship for Americans' political engagement. Citizenship norms are shifting from a pattern of duty-based citizenship to engaged citizenship. Using data from the 2005 'Citizenship, Involvement, Democracy' survey of the Center for Democracy and Civil Society (CDACS) I describe these two faces of citizenship, and trace their impact on political participation. Rather than the erosion of participation, this norm shift is altering and expanding the patterns of political participation in America.
(Dalton, R.J. (2008) *Political Studies* 56 (1) 76–98)

Abstracts normally have a standard structure.

■ **Underline the main components of the abstract above.**

(a) Background position

(b) Aim and thesis of article

(c) Method of research

(d) Results of research

4 Fact and opinion

When reading, it is important to distinguish between facts:

Rice is grown in warm wet climates.

and opinions:

I like rice.

■ **Decide if the following statements are facts, opinions or both.**

	Fact	Opinion
1 Smoking can be dangerous to health.		
2 Smoking is addictive.		
3 Smoking should be banned.		
4 Smoking is dangerous so it should be banned.		

If suggestions are made in academic writing (smoking should be banned) it is important that they are supported by true facts (smoking is dangerous).

■ **Read the following sentences and decide if they are fact or opinion. If they are fact, decide if they are true or false. If they are opinion, decide if you agree or disagree.**

	Fact or opinion?	Facts – true or false?	Opinions – agree or disagree?
1 Britain has the highest crime rate in the world.			
2 In Britain, hundreds of crimes are committed every day.			
3 Many criminals are never caught.			
4 The police are inefficient.			
5 The police should be abolished.			

5 Assessing internet sources critically

You cannot afford to waste time on texts that are unreliable or out-of-date. If you are using material that is not on the reading list you must assess it critically to ensure that the material is trustworthy. Internet sources are plentiful and conveniently available, but you need to ask several questions about each site:

• Is this a reputable website, for example with ac. (= academic) in the URL?

• Is the name of the author given, and is he/she well-known in the field?

• Is the language of the text in a suitable academic style?

• Are there any obvious errors in the text, e.g. spelling mistakes, which suggest a careless approach?

■ **Compare these two internet texts on deforestation. Which is likely to be more reliable?**

5.1 We are destroying the last of our vital natural resources, just as we are starting to wake up to how precious they are. Rainforest once covered 14 per cent of the land now it's down to a mere 6 per cent. Scientists predict that the rest could disappear in less than 40 years. Thousands of acres are cut down each second with dire consequences for the countries involved and the planet as a whole. Scientists estimate that we loose 50,000 species every year, many species every second including 137 plant types (not even species but whole groups of plant species) and as these plants disappear before science can record them so does the chance to gain helpful knowledge and possible medicines.

5.2 The scale of human pressures on ecosystems everywhere has increased enormously in the last few decades. Since 1980 the global economy has tripled in size and the world population has increased by 30 per cent. Consumption of everything on the planet has risen – at a cost to our ecosystems. In 2001, The World Resources Institute estimated that the demand for rice, wheat, and corn is expected to grow by 40 per cent by 2020, increasing irrigation water demands by 50 per cent or more. They further reported that the demand for wood could double by the year 2050; unfortunately it is still the tropical forests that supply the bulk of the world's demand for wood.

There are several aspects of (1) which should make the reader cautious: the style is very personal (we are . . .) and informal (it's down to . . .) and there is a word used wrongly ('loose' instead of 'lose'). No sources are provided. But possibly more disturbing is carelessness with facts. Is it really possible that thousands of acres of rainforest are being cut down *every second*? The writer also claims that many species are being lost *every second*, but if we take the figure of 50,000 per year it means one species is lost every 10 minutes. Clearly the writer is seeking to dramatise the subject, but it is quite unsuitable as an academic source.

In contrast, the second text is written in accurate, semi-formal language and includes a source. It seems more likely to be reliable.

6 Practice

■ (a) Read the following texts and decide if you can trust the information. Give reasons for your decisions in the table below.

6.1 Hard up? Why struggle when you could live in luxury? Solve your money worries easily and quickly by working for us. No experience needed, you can earn hundreds of pounds for just a few hours' work per day. Work when it suits you, day or night. Don't delay, call today for an interview on 07795–246791.

6.2 If you have money problems, there's lots of ways you can save cash. Instead of spending money on new clothes, try buying them secondhand from charity shops, where you'll find lots of stylish bargains. Eating out is another big expense, but instead you can get together with a few friends and cook a meal together; it's cheaper and it's fun. Bus fares and taxis can also cost a lot, so it might be worth looking for a cheap bicycle, which lets you travel where you want, when you want.

6.3 Most students find that they have financial difficulties at times. It has been estimated that nearly 55 per cent experience financial difficulties in their first year at college or university. It's often hard living on a small fixed income, and the cost of accommodation and food can come as a shock when you first live away from your parents. The most important thing, if you find you are getting into debt, is to speak to a financial advisor in the Student Union, who may be able to help you sort out your problems.

1	
2	
3	

■ (b) You are writing an essay on expanding educational provision in developing countries, titled:

'Improving literacy in sub-Saharan Africa.'

■ You find the following article in a recent magazine. Read it critically and decide whether you could use it in your work.

6.4 How can we get the world's poorest children into school? This is a difficult question with no easy answer. In 1999 the UN adopted a set of goals called 'Education for All', but in many countries there has been little progress towards these aims. In Nigeria, for instance, the number of children not going to school has hardly changed since then. It is estimated that worldwide about 72m children never attend school, 45 per cent of whom are in sub-Saharan Africa. Even when schools and teachers are provided, there's no guarantee that teaching is going on: World Bank research in India shows that a quarter of teachers don't turn up on any day. Several proposals have been made to improve matters. A British academic, Professor Tooley, argues that low-cost private schools are more effective in delivering education to the poor since parental pressure maintains good standards. State schools could also relate pay to performance: research by Muralihadan and Sundararaman in India found that this improved students' test performance far more significantly than spending the same money on teaching materials.

Positive aspects: _____

_____

Negative aspects: _____

_____

7 Critical thinking

Even when you feel that a text is reliable and that you can safely use it as a source, it is still important to adopt a critical attitude towards it. This approach is perhaps easiest to learn when reading, but is important for all other academic work (i.e. listening, discussing and writing). Critical thinking means not just passively accepting what you hear or read, but instead actively questioning and assessing it. As you read you should ask yourself the following questions:

(a) What are the key ideas in this?

(b) Does the argument of the writer develop logically, step by step?

(c) Are the examples given helpful? Would other examples be better?

(d) Does the author have any bias?

(e) Does the evidence presented seem reliable, in my experience and using common sense?

(f) Is this argument similar to anything else I have read?

(g) Do I agree with the writer's views?

■ **Read the following text (7.1), thinking critically about the sections in bold. Then answer questions 1–9.**

7.1   The growth of the world wide web

In the history of civilisation there have been many significant developments, **such as the invention of the wheel, money and the telephone,** but **the development of the internet is perhaps the most crucial of all**. In the space of a few years the world wide web has linked buyers in New York to sellers in Mumbai and teachers in Berlin to students in Cairo, **so that few people can imagine life without it.**

It is estimated that over 70 per cent of North Americans, for instance, have internet access, and this figure is steadily increasing. **Physical shops are under threat, as growing numbers shop online.** In areas such as travel it is now impossible to buy tickets on certain airlines except on the internet. The web also links together millions of individual traders who sell to buyers through websites such as Ebay.

Beyond the commercial sphere, the internet is also critically important in the academic world. A huge range of journals and reports are now available electronically, meaning that researchers can access a vast amount of information through their computer screens, **speeding up their work and allowing them to produce better quality research**. In addition, email permits academics to make effortless contact with fellow-researchers all over the world, which also assists them to improve their output.

There is, of course, a darker side to this phenomenon, which is the use criminals have made of their ability to trade illegal or fraudulent products over the internet, with little control over their activities. But such behaviour is hugely compensated for by the benefits that have been obtained by both individuals and businesses. **We are reaching a situation in which all kinds of information are freely available to everyone, which must lead to a happier, healthier and richer society.**

1   '... such as the invention of the wheel, money and the
    telephone ...'

    Are these really critical developments?

2   '... the development of the internet is perhaps the most
    crucial of all.'

    Is this true?

3   '... so that few people can imagine life without it.'

    Is this claim credible?

4   'It is estimated that over 70 per cent of North Americans, for
    instance, have internet access ...'

    No source given. Does this figure seem likely?

5   'Physical shops are under threat, as growing numbers shop
    online.'

    Is the first part true, and if so, is it caused by online shopping?

6   '... speeding up their work and allowing them to produce
    better quality research.'

    If the first part is true, does the result logically follow?

7   'We are reaching a situation in which all kinds of information
    are freely available to everyone, which must lead to a happier,
    healthier and richer society.'

    Does the first part need any qualification?

    Is the conclusion justified?

8   Is the writer objective or biased?

9   Do I agree with this argument overall?

@   Critical thinking>

▶   See Unit 2.1 Argument and discussion

Avoiding plagiarism

In the English-speaking academic world it is essential to use a wide range of sources for your writing, and to acknowledge these sources clearly. This unit explains why this is vital, and introduces the techniques students need to use. Further practice with these is provided in Units 1.6 Paraphrasing, 1.7 Summarising and 1.8 References and quotations.

1 What is plagiarism?

Basically plagiarism means taking ideas or words from a source without giving credit (acknowledgement) to the author. It is seen as a kind of theft, and is considered to be an academic crime. In academic work, ideas and words are seen as private property belonging to the person who first thought or wrote them. Therefore it is important for all students, including international ones, to understand the meaning of plagiarism and learn how to prevent it in their work.

The main difficulty that students face is that they are expected:

(a) to show that they have read the principal experts on a subject – by giving citations

(b) to explain these ideas in their own words and come to their own original conclusions

There are several reasons why students must avoid plagiarism:

*   Copying the work of others will not help you develop your own understanding

*   To show that you understand the rules of the academic community

*   Plagiarism is easily detected by teachers and computer software

*   It may lead to failing a course or even having to leave college

2 Acknowledging sources

If you borrow from or refer to the work of another person, you must show that you have done this by providing the correct acknowledgement. There are two ways to do this:

Summary and citation
Smith (2009) claims that the modern state wields power in new ways.

Quotation and citation
According to Smith: 'The point is not that the state is in retreat but that it is developing new forms of power . . .' (Smith, 2009: 103).

These in-text **citations** are linked to a list of **references** at the end of the main text, which includes the following details:

Author	Date	Title	Place of publication	Publisher
Smith, M.	(2009)	*Power and the State*	Basingstoke	Palgrave Macmillan

The citation makes it clear to the reader that you have read Smith and borrowed this idea from him. This reference gives the reader the necessary information to find the source if the reader needs more detail.

▶ **See Unit 1.8 References and quotations**

3 Degrees of plagiarism

Although plagiarism essentially means copying somebody else's work, it is not always easy to define.

■ **Working with a partner, consider the following academic situations and decide if they are plagiarism.**

	Situation	Yes/No
1	Copying a paragraph, but changing a few words and giving a citation.	*Yes*
2	Cutting and pasting a short article from a website, with no citation.	
3	Taking two paragraphs from a classmate's essay, without citation.	
4	Taking a graph from a textbook, giving the source.	
5	Taking a quotation from a source, giving a citation but not using quotation marks.	
6	Using something that you think of as general knowledge, e.g. large areas of rainforest have been cut down in recent years.	
7	Using a paragraph from an essay you wrote and had marked the previous semester, without citation.	
8	Using the results of your own research, e.g. from a survey, without citation.	
9	Discussing an essay topic with a group of classmates and using some of their ideas in your own work.	
10	Giving a citation for some information but mis-spelling the author's name.	

This exercise shows that plagiarism can be accidental. For example, situation (10) above, when the author's name is mis-spelt, is technically plagiarism but really carelessness. In situation (9) your teacher may have encouraged you to discuss the topic in groups, and then write an essay on your own, in which case it would not be plagiarism. Self-plagiarism is also theoretically possible, as in situation (7). It can be difficult to decide what is general or common knowledge (situation 6), but you can always try asking colleagues.

However, it is not a good excuse to say that you didn't know the rules of plagiarism, or that you didn't have time to write in your own words. Nor is it adequate to say that the rules are different in your own country. In general, anything that is not common knowledge or your own ideas and research (published or not) must be cited and referenced.

4 Avoiding plagiarism by summarising and paraphrasing

Quotations should not be over-used, so you must learn to paraphrase and summarise in order to include other writers' ideas in your work. This will demonstrate your understanding of a text to your teachers.

- Paraphrasing involves re-writing a text so that the language is substantially different while the content stays the same.

- Summarising means reducing the length of a text but retaining the main points.

▶ **See Units 1.6 Paraphrasing and 1.7 Summarising**

Normally both skills are used at the same time, as can be seen in the examples below.

■ **Read the following text and then compare the five paragraphs below, which use ideas and information from it. Decide which are plagiarised and which are acceptable, and give your reasons in the table.**

4.1 **RAILWAY MANIAS**

In 1830 there were a few dozen miles of railways in all the world – chiefly consisting of the line from Liverpool to Manchester. By 1840 there were over 4,500 miles, by 1850 over 23,500. Most of them were projected in a few bursts of speculative frenzy known as the 'railway manias' of 1835–7 and especially in 1844–7; most of them were built in large part with British capital, British iron, machines and know-how. These investment booms appear irrational, because in fact few railways were much more profitable to the investor than other forms of enterprise, most yielded quite modest profits and many none at all: in 1855 the average interest on capital sunk in the British railways was a mere 3.7 per cent.

(From *The Age of Revolution* by Eric Hobsbawm, 1995, p. 45)

(a) Between 1830 and 1850 there was very rapid development in railway construction worldwide. Two periods of especially feverish growth were 1835–7 and 1844–7. It is hard to understand the reason for this intense activity, since railways were not particularly profitable investments and some produced no return at all. (Hobsbawm, 1995: 45)

(b) There were only a few dozen miles of railways in 1830, including the Liverpool to Manchester line. But by 1840 there were over 4,500 miles and over 23,500 by 1850. Most of them were built in large part with British capital, British iron, machines and know-how, and most of them were projected in a few bursts of speculative frenzy known as the 'railway manias' of 1835–7 and especially in 1844–7. Because most yielded quite modest profits and many none at all these investment booms appear irrational. In fact few railways were much more profitable to the investor than other forms of enterprise. (Hobsbawm, 1995: 45)

(c) As Hobsbawm (1995) argues, nineteenth-century railway mania was partly irrational: 'because in fact few railways were much more profitable to the investor than other forms of enterprise, most yielded quite modest profits and many none at all: in 1855 the average interest on capital sunk in the British railways was a mere 3.7 per cent.' (Hobsbawm, 1995: 45)

(d) Globally, railway networks increased dramatically from 1830 to 1850; the majority in short periods of 'mania' (1835–7 and 1844–7). British technology and capital were responsible for much of this growth, yet the returns on the investment were hardly any better than comparable business opportunities. (Hobsbawm, 1895: 45)

(e) The dramatic growth of railways between 1830 and 1850 was largely achieved using British technology. However, it has been claimed that much of this development was irrational because few railways were much more profitable to the investor than other forms of enterprise; most yielded quite modest profits and many none at all.

	Plagiarised or acceptable?
a	
b	
c	
d	
e	

5 Avoiding plagiarism by developing good study habits

Few students deliberately try to cheat by plagiarising, but some develop poor study habits that result in the risk of plagiarism.

■ **Working with a partner, add to the list of positive habits.**

- Plan your work carefully so you don't have to write the essay at the last minute.

- Take care to make notes in your own words, not copying from the source.

- Keep a record of all the sources you use (e.g. author, date, title, page numbers, publisher).

- Make sure your in-text citations are all included in the list of references.

- _____

- _____

6 Research

Does your college or university have a policy on plagiarism? Look on the website to find out. It may raise some issues that you want to discuss with colleagues or your teachers.

If you can't find anything for your institution try one of these sites:

http://owl.english.purdue.edu/owl/resource/589/01/
http://uefap.com/writing/plagiar/plagfram.htm

CHAPTER 1

From understanding titles to planning

In both exams and coursework it is essential for students to understand what an essay title is asking them to do. A plan can then be prepared, which should ensure the question is answered fully, while preventing time being wasted. This unit looks at:

- key words in titles
- brainstorming ideas
- alternative methods of essay planning

1 The planning process

Although teachers frequently complain that students do not answer the question set, this problem can be avoided by more care at the start of the process. Planning is necessary with all academic writing, but clearly there are important differences between planning in exams, when time is short, and for coursework, when preparatory reading is required. However, in both cases the process of planning should include these three steps:

(a) Analyse the title wording and decide what is required.

(b) Brainstorm the topic to focus your ideas.

(c) Prepare an outline using your preferred method.

With coursework your outline will probably be revised as you read around the topic.

▶ **See Unit 4.5 Writing longer essays**

2 Analysing essay titles

Titles contain key words that tell the student what to do. Note that titles often have two (or more) parts:

'**What** is meant by a demand curve and **why** would we expect it to slope downwards?'

In this case 'what' is asking for a description and 'why' for a reason or explanation.

■ **Match the key words on the left to the definitions on the right.**

Analyse	Explain a topic briefly and clearly
Assess (Evaluate)	Deal with a complex subject by reducing it to the main elements
Describe	Divide into sections and discuss each critically
Discuss	**Break down into the various parts and their relationships**
Examine (Explore)	Make a proposal and support it
Illustrate	Look at various aspects of a topic, compare benefits and drawbacks
Outline (Trace)	Give a detailed account of something
State	Give a simple, basic account of the main points of a topic
Suggest	Give examples
Summarise	Decide the value or worth of a subject

3 Practice

■ **Underline the key words in the following titles and consider what they are asking you to do.**

(a) How and why has the market for international tourism segmented since the middle of the twentieth century? What are the economic and social forces that have driven this process?

(b) Describe some of the reasons why patients do not always take their medication as directed.

(c) How can psychology contribute to the reduction of bullying behaviour in schools?

(d) Is there a move towards subjectivity in criminal law? Should there be?

(e) Discuss the response of buildings and soil to earthquakes, indicating what measures can be used to ensure structural stability.

4 Brainstorming

It is often helpful to start thinking about a topic by writing down any ideas you have, in any order. Taking the example from (3a), you might collect the following points:

International tourism – segmentation of market

How and why:

• Package holidays made foreign holidays popular
• Internet allows travellers to plan own holidays
• In 60s jet aircraft permit faster travel – long and short haul holidays
• In 90s budget airlines lower costs – short breaks

Economic and political forces:

• Rising disposable incomes permit more spending on travel
• Developing countries see tourism as route to growth
• Older, retired people spend more on travel

■ **Working with a partner, brainstorm ideas for the title below.**

> *What are the benefits of learning a second language at primary school (age 6-10)? Are there any drawbacks to early language learning?*

5 Essay length

Coursework essays usually have a required length, normally between 1,000 and 5,000 words. You must keep to this limit, although deviations of 5 per cent more or less are generally acceptable. However, at the planning stage you need to consider what proportion of the essay to allocate to each part of the question.

As a basic guide, 20 per cent is usually sufficient for the introduction and conclusion together (references are not included in the word count). Therefore, in a 2,000 word essay the main body would have 1,600 words.

If this was the length given for title (3a) above, you might decide on the following allocation:

Segmentation of the market for international tourism – how	300 words
– why	500 words
Economic forces	400 words
Social forces	400 words
Total	**1,600 words**

This calculation is useful since it can guide the amount of reading you need to do, as well as providing the basis for an outline. Moreover, it prevents you from writing an unbalanced answer, in which part of the question is not fully dealt with.

Essays in exams do not have a word limit, but it is equally important to plan them in similar terms, e.g. part 1 40 per cent, part 2 60 per cent.

■ **Identify the key words in the following titles and decide what percentage of the main body to give to each part.**

Title	Part 1 (%)	Part 2 (%)
(a) Describe the typical social, cultural and environmental impacts experienced by tourist destinations in developing countries. How can harmful impacts be reduced or avoided?		
(b) How can schools make better use of IT (information technology)? Illustrate your answer with examples.		
(c) Outline the main difficulties in combating malaria. Suggest possible strategies for more effective anti-malaria campaigns.		
(d) What is 'donor fatigue' in international aid and how can it be overcome?		

6 Outlines

An outline should help the writer to answer the question as effectively as possible. Care at this stage will save wasted effort later. The more detail you include in your outline, the easier the writing process will be. Note that for coursework it is usually better to write the main body first, then the introduction and finally the conclusion. Therefore you may prefer to outline just the main body at this stage.

There is no fixed pattern for an outline; different methods appeal to different students. For example, with first part of title (5a) above:

'Describe the typical social, cultural and environmental impacts experienced by tourist destinations in developing countries.'

(a) The outline might be a list:

  (i) Social impacts
    •   increase in variety of jobs available
    •   price inflation
    •   new range of business opportunities

  (ii) Cultural impacts
    •   new patterns of dress and behaviour may cause
         problems
    •   market for traditional crafts and/or rituals grows

  (iii) Environmental impacts
    •   increased pressure on limited resources, e.g. water
    •   loss of natural habitat to building projects
    •   provision of new infrastructure, e.g. roads

(b) An alternative is a mind map:

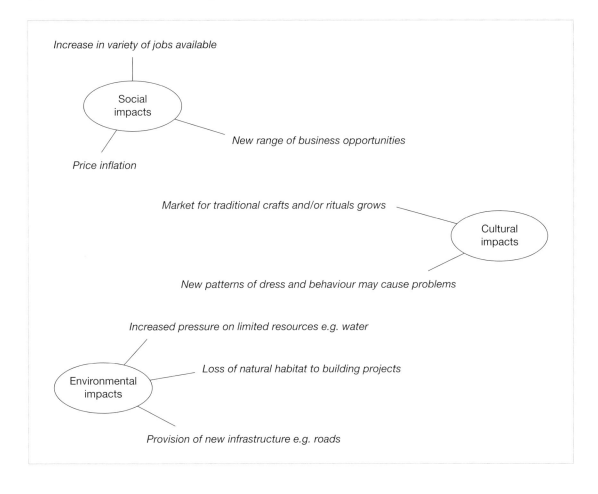

■ (i) What are the advantages and drawbacks of each method?

■ (ii) Prepare an outline for the second part of the same title, using either method:

'How can harmful impacts be reduced or avoided?'

Outline

Finding key points and note-making

After finding a suitable source and identifying relevant sections of text, the next step is to select the key points that relate to your topic and make notes on them. This unit explains and practises this process, which also involves skills developed in Units 1.6 Paraphrasing and 1.7 Summarising.

1 Why make notes?

■ What are the main reasons for note-making? Add to the list below.

(a) _To prepare for essay writing_ _____

(b) _____

(c) _____

(d) _____

(e) _____

2 Note-making methods

■ You are looking for information on the current media revolution.
Study the text below (key points underlined) and the notes in the box.
What do you notice about the language of the notes?

2.1   **THE DEATH OF THE PRESS?**

<u>A hundred years ago news was exclusively provided by newspapers</u>. There was no other way of supplying the latest information on politics, crime, finance or sport to the millions of people who bought and read newspapers, sometimes twice a day. <u>Today</u> the situation is very different. <u>The same news is also available on television, radio and the internet</u>, and because of the nature of these media, can be more up-to-date than in print. For young people especially, the internet has become the natural source of news and comment.

<u>This development means that in many countries newspaper circulation is falling, and a loss of readers also means a fall in advertising, which is the main income for most papers. Consequently, in both Britain and the USA newspapers are closing every week</u>. But when a local newspaper goes out of business an important part of the community is lost. It allows debate on local issues, as well as providing a noticeboard for events such as weddings and society meetings.

All newspapers are concerned by these developments, and <u>many have tried to find methods of increasing their sales. One approach is to focus on magazine-type articles</u> rather than news, <u>another is to give free gifts</u> such as DVDs, while <u>others have developed their own websites</u> to provide continuous news coverage. However, as so much is now freely available online to anyone with a web browser, <u>none of these have had a significant impact</u> on the steady decline of paid-for newspapers.

(Source: *New Business Monthly*, May 2010, p. 37)

Decline of newspapers   (*New Business Monthly*, May 2010, p. 37)

a) Newspapers only source of news 100 yrs ago – now also TV, radio + www

b) Newspaper sales   > decline in advertising > newspapers shutting

c) Attempts to increase sales: – more magazine content
                                                            – gifts
                                                            – websites

                                but none effective.

---

3 Finding key points

■ Read the following text and underline two key points. Then choose a
  title for the paragraph.

Title: _____

3.1   The generation born after the second world war,
            sometimes called the baby-boomers, are now reaching
retirement age, and businesses are starting to realise that they
are a wealthier market than any previous retirement group.
Financial products, travel and medicines are well-established
industries which interest the over-60s, but others are now
focusing on this age group. Volkswagen, for instance, has
produced a car with raised seats and more interior space to
appeal to their tastes. In Japan, with its ageing population,
companies have more experience of selling to the retired, and
have been successful with unusual products such as a robotic
seal, which serves as a pet substitute for the lonely. There are,
however, certain difficulties in selling to this market. Some
customers resent being addressed as 'old' since they see
themselves as more youthful, while there is a huge variation in
the profile of the baby boomers, ranging from healthy and
active to the bed-ridden and infirm.

4 Finding relevant points

When preparing to write an essay you have to search for information and
ideas relevant to your subject. Therefore the key points that you select
must relate to that topic.

You are given an essay title:

> 'Does the state have a role in promoting public health?'

■ **Read the following article and underline the key points that relate to
your essay topic.**

4.1   A SLIMMER AMERICA?

Currently over two-thirds of Americans are believed to be either overweight or
obese, but recently it has been discovered that the situation may have stabilised.
The rate of increase appears to have virtually stopped, so that on average women
and children weigh no more now than they did ten years ago. This trend may have
important consequences for the health care system: according to a recent study
(Finkelstein *et al.*, 2009) an obese American is likely to cost the system over
40 per cent more than someone with normal weight. This is due to the increased
risks of medical conditions such as diabetes, to which should be added extra costs
connected with illness and resulting absence from work.

Until recently it was assumed that the long-term trend would continue so that
ultimately all Americans would become overweight; Wang (2008) had estimated
that this would happen by 2048. Obviously, such an assumption implies steadily
rising medical insurance costs. If the new trend continues there are clear benefits
for public health and the associated finances, but medical researchers still struggle
to understand the basic causes of the problem, which is that obesity in America is
now three times greater than fifty years ago.

There is substantial evidence that obesity is linked to social class: those with
irregular and badly paid employment are more likely to eat what is convenient and
tasty rather than have the time or energy to organise a healthy diet. The number
of people in this category may have risen in recent years. Another possibility is
that food now is cheaper relative to income, while free time is more valuable, so

---

continued . . .

> **cont.** people are attracted to consuming convenient but often unhealthy fast
> food. In addition, washing machines and other devices mean that fewer
> calories are used in doing domestic chores around the house. Although valid,
> these factors apply in many other countries where the same growth in obesity
> has not been seen.
>
> Recent years have certainly seen more pressure for informative food labelling
> and campaigns to encourage school children to eat more fruit and vegetables.
> Although Americans often dislike being told what to do by their government,
> these campaigns may finally be having an effect. Certainly about a third of the
> population attempt a slimming programme every year, and although many give
> up it appears that the number of people who succeed may be rising.
>
> (Herapath, T. (2010) *Journal of Transatlantic Contexts* 14, 319)

5 Effective note-making

Notes are for your personal use so you should create your own style.

(a) You must use your own words and not copy phrases from the original
   to avoid the risk of plagiarism. The quantity of notes you make depends
   on your task: you may only need a few points, or a lot of detail.

(b) Always record the source of your notes, to save time when you have
   to write the list of references.

(c) Notes are written quickly, so keep them simple. Do not write sentences.
   Leave out articles (a/ the) and prepositions (of/ to).

(d) If you write lists, it is important to have clear headings (underlined)
   and numbering systems (a, b, c, or 1, 2, 3,) to organise the information.
   Do not crowd your notes.

(e) Use symbols (+, >, =) to save time.

(f) Use abbreviations (e.g. = for example). You need to make up your
   own abbreviations for your subject area. But do not abbreviate too
   much, or you may find your notes hard to understand in the future!

▶ **See Unit 3.1 Abbreviations**

6 Practice A

■ Complete the notes for 'Does the state have a role in promoting public health?' using the key points underlined in (4) above.

Source: (Herapath, T. (2010) *Journal of Transatlantic Contexts* 14, 319)

<u>Have Americans stopped getting fatter?</u>

(1) *2/3 Americans overweight, but lately growth in obesity seems to have stopped*

(2) *May reduce future healthcare costs (obesity adds 40 per cent to medical expenses – Finkelstein et al., 2009)*

(3)

(4)

(5)

---

7 Practice B

You have to write an essay titled:

'Improving student performance: an outline of recent research.'

■ Read the following text and make notes on the relevant key points.

7.1 SLEEP AND MEMORY

In many countries, especially in hot climates, it is the custom to take a short sleep in the afternoon, often known as a siesta. Now it appears that this habit helps to improve the ability to remember and therefore to learn. Researchers have known for some time that new memories are stored short-term in an area of the brain called the hippocampus, but are then transferred to the pre-frontal cortex for

continued . . .

cont. long-term storage. They now believe that this transfer process occurs during a kind of sleep called stage 2 non-REM sleep. After this has occurred the brain is better able to take in new information, and having a sleep of about 100 minutes after lunch seems to be an effective way to permit this.

Research by a team from the University of California sought to confirm this theory. They wanted to establish that a short sleep would restore the brain's ability to learn. A group of about 40 people were asked to take part in two 'lessons'; at 12 noon and 6 pm. Half the volunteers were put in a group which stayed awake all day, while the others were encouraged to sleep for an hour and a half after the first session. It was found that in the second lesson the second group were better at remembering what they had learnt, which indicates that the siesta had helped to refresh their short-term memories.

The most effective siesta seems to consist of three parts: roughly 30 minutes of light sleep to rest the body, followed by 30 minutes of stage 2 sleep which clears the hippocampus, and finally 30 minutes of REM sleep which is when dreams are experienced: possibly as a result of the new memories being processed as they are stored in the pre-frontal cortex. This process is believed to be so valuable that some researchers argue that a siesta can be as beneficial as a full night's sleep.

(Kitschelt, P. (2006) *How the Brain Works.* Berlin: Freihaus, p.73)

@ Note-making>

Paraphrasing

Paraphrasing means changing the wording of a text so that it is significantly different from the original source, without changing the meaning. Effective paraphrasing is a key academic skill needed to avoid the risk of plagiarism: it demonstrates your understanding of a source. This unit focuses on techniques for paraphrasing as part of the note-making and summarising process.

1 The elements of effective paraphrasing

Paraphrasing and summarising are normally used together in essay writing, but while summarising aims to **reduce** information to a suitable length, paraphrasing attempts to **restate** the relevant information. For example, the following sentence:

> There has been much debate about the reasons for the industrial revolution happening in eighteenth-century Britain, rather than in France or Germany.

could be paraphrased:

> Why the industrial revolution occurred in Britain in the eighteenth century, instead of on the continent, has been the subject of considerable discussion.

Note that an effective paraphrase usually:

- has a different structure to the original

- has mainly different vocabulary

- retains the same meaning

- keeps some phrases from the original that are in common use
  e.g. 'industrial revolution' or 'eighteenth century'

2 Practice A

■ **Read the text below and then evaluate the three paraphrases (1=best),
giving reasons.**

2.1   **THE CAUSES OF THE INDUSTRIAL
REVOLUTION**

Allen (2009) argues that the best explanation for the British
location of the industrial revolution is found by studying
demand factors. By the early eighteenth century high wages
and cheap energy were both features of the British economy.
Consequently, the mechanisation of industry through such
inventions as the steam engine and mechanical spinning was
profitable because employers were able to economise on
labour by spending on coal. At that time, no other country
had this particular combination of expensive labour and
abundant fuel.

(a) A focus on demand may help to explain the UK origin of the
industrial revolution. At that time workers' pay was high, but
energy from coal was inexpensive. This encouraged the
development of mechanical inventions based on steam power,
which enabled bosses to save money by mechanising
production (Allen, 2009).

(b) The reason why Britain was the birthplace of the industrial
revolution can be understood by analysing demand in the
early 1700s, according to Allen (2009). He maintains that,

uniquely, Britain had the critical combination of cheap energy from coal and high labour costs. This encouraged the adoption of steam power to mechanise production, thus saving on wages and increasing profitability.

(c) Allen (2009) claims that the clearest explanation for the UK location of the industrial revolution is seen by examining demand factors. By the eighteenth century cheap energy and high wages were both aspects of the British economy. As a result, the mechanisation of industry through inventions such as the steam engine and mechanical spinning was profitable because employers were able to save money on employees by spending on coal. At that time, Britain was the only country with significant deposits of coal.

a	
b	
c	

3 Techniques for paraphrasing

(a) Changing vocabulary by using synonyms:

argues > claims/ eighteenth century > 1700s/ wages > labour costs/ economise > saving

NB. Do not attempt to paraphrase every word, since some have no true synonym, e.g. demand, economy, energy

(b) Changing word class:

explanation (n.) > explain (v.) / mechanical (adj.) > mechanise (v.) / profitable (adj.) > profitability (n.)

(c) Changing word order:

. . . the best explanation for the British location of the industrial revolution is found by studying demand factors.

> A focus on demand may help explain the UK origin of the industrial revolution.

▶ **See Units 3.2 Academic vocabulary and 3.11 Synonyms**

4 Practice B

■ **Read the following text and then practise the techniques illustrated above.**

4.1   **FOUR WHEELS GOOD**

The growth of the car industry parallels the development of modern capitalism. It began in France and Germany, but took off in the United States. There Henry Ford adapted the moving production line from the Chicago meat industry to motor manufacturing, thus inventing mass production. In the 1920s Alfred Sloan's management theories helped General Motors to become the world's dominant car company. After the second world war the car makers focused on the styling of their products to encourage more frequent model changes. From the 1970s there was criticism of the industry due to the inefficiency of most vehicles, which used petrol wastefully. At the same time, trades unions became increasingly militant in defence of their members' jobs. Today the industry owns some of the most famous brands in the world. However, many car makers are currently threatened by increased competition and saturated markets.

■ **(a) Find synonyms for the words underlined.**

(i) The <u>growth</u> of the <u>car</u> industry <u>parallels</u> the <u>development</u> of <u>modern</u> capitalism.

    Example: The <u>rise</u> of the <u>automobile</u> industry <u>matches</u> the <u>progress</u> of <u>contemporary</u> capitalism.

(ii) It <u>began</u> in France and Germany, but <u>took off</u> in the United States.

(iii) There Henry Ford <u>adapted</u> the moving <u>production</u> line from the Chicago meat industry to <u>motor</u> manufacturing, <u>thus</u> inventing mass production.

■ **(b) Change the word class of the underlined words, and then re-write the sentences.**

(i) In the 1920s Alfred Sloan's <u>management</u> theories <u>helped</u> General Motors to become the world's <u>dominant</u> car company.

Example: In the 1920s, with help from the managerial theories of Alfred Sloan, General Motors dominated the world's car companies.

(ii) After the second world war the car makers <u>focused</u> on the <u>styling</u> of their products, to encourage more frequent model changes.

(iii) From the 1970s there was <u>criticism</u> of the industry due to the <u>inefficiency</u> of most vehicles, which used petrol <u>wastefully</u>.

■ **(c) Change the word order of the following sentences (other changes may be needed).**

(i) At the same time, trades unions became increasingly militant in defence of their members' jobs.

Example: At the same time increasingly militant trades unions defended their members' jobs.

(ii) Today the industry owns some of the most famous brands in the world.

(iii) However, many car makers are currently threatened by increased competition and saturated markets.

■ **(d) Combine all these techniques to paraphrase the paragraph as fully as possible.**

5 Practice C

■ Use the same techniques to paraphrase the following text.

5.1 THE PAST BELOW THE WAVES

More than three million shipwrecks are believed to lie on the seabed, the result of storms and accidents during thousands of years of sea-borne trading. These wrecks offer marine archaeologists valuable information about the culture, technology and trade patterns of ancient civilisations, but the vast majority have been too deep to research. Scuba divers can only operate down to 50 metres, which limits operations to wrecks near the coast, which have often been damaged by storms or plant growth. A few deep sea sites (such as the *Titanic*) have been explored by manned submarines, but this kind of equipment has been too expensive for less famous subjects. However, this situation has been changed by the introduction of a new kind of mini submarine: the automatic underwater vehicle (AUV). This cheap, small craft is free moving and does not need an expensive mother-ship to control it. Now a team of American archaeologists are planning to use an AUV to explore an area of sea north of Egypt which was the approach to a major trading port 4,000 years ago.

@ Paraphrasing>

Summarising

Making oral summaries is a common activity, for example when describing a film or a book. In academic writing it is a vital skill, allowing the writer to condense lengthy sources into a concise form. Like most skills it becomes easier with practice, and this unit explains the basic steps needed to achieve an accurate summary.

1 What makes a good summary?

■ Write a summary of one of the topics below in no more than 20 words.

(a) One of your parents

(b) A town or city you know well

(c) A film you have recently watched

■ Compare your summary with others in your class. What is needed for a good summary?

• _____

• _____

• _____

2 Stages of summarising

Summarising is a flexible tool. You can use it to give a one-sentence synopsis of an article, or to provide much more detail, depending on your writing needs. But in every case the same basic steps need to be followed in order to meet the criteria discussed in (1).

■ Study the stages of summary writing below, which have been mixed up. Put them in the correct order.

(a) Write the summary from your notes, re-organising the structure if needed.

(b) Make notes of the key points, paraphrasing where possible.

(c) Read the original text carefully and check any new or difficult vocabulary.

(d) Mark the key points by underlining or highlighting.

(e) Check the summary to ensure it is accurate and nothing important has been changed or lost.

3 Practice A

■ Read the following text (3.1) and the summaries (a)–(c). Rate them 1 (best) – 3.

(a) Fruit crops have usually been picked by hand, as it is difficult to mechanise the process. But in rich countries it has become hard to find affordable pickers at the right time so fruit is often wasted. Therefore intelligent machines have been developed that can overcome the technical problems involved, and also provide the farmer with useful data about the plants.

3.1　MECHANICAL PICKERS

Although harvesting cereal crops such as wheat and barley has long been done by large machines known as combine harvesters, mechanising the picking of fruit crops such as tomatoes or apples has proved more difficult. Farmers have generally relied on human labour to harvest these, but in wealthy countries it has become increasingly difficult to find pickers willing to work for the wages farmers are able to pay. This is partly because the demand for labour is seasonal, usually in the autumn, and also because the work is hard and demanding. As a result, in areas such as California part of the fruit harvest is often unpicked and left to rot.

There are several obvious reasons why developing mechanical pickers is challenging. Fruit such as grapes or strawberries comes in a variety of shapes and does not always ripen at the same time. Outdoors, the ground conditions can vary from dry to muddy, and winds may move branches around. Clearly each crop requires its own solution: machines may be towed through orchards by tractors or move around by themselves using sensors to detect the ripest fruit.

This new generation of fruit harvesters is possible due to advances in computing power and sensing ability. Such devices will inevitably be expensive, but will save farmers from the complexities of managing a labour force. In addition, the more intelligent pickers should be able to develop a database of information on the health of each individual plant, enabling the grower to provide it with fertiliser and water to maintain its maximum productivity.

(b) Developing machines that can pick fruit such as tomatoes or apples is a challenging task, due to the complexity of locating ripe fruit in an unpredictable outdoor environment, where difficult conditions can be produced by wind or water. But recent developments in computing ability mean that growers can now automate this process, which should save them money and increase their profits.

(c) Strawberries and grapes are the kind of crops that have always been hand-picked. But many farmers, for example in California, now find it increasingly difficult to attract enough pickers when the fruit is ripe. However, computing advances have produced a solution to this problem, which will save farmers from worrying about the pickers, and also collect vital data.

4 Practice B

■ **Read the following text and underline the key points.**

4.1   WEALTH AND FERTILITY

For most of the past century an inverse correlation between human fertility and economic development has been found. This means that as a country got richer, the average number of children born to each woman got smaller. While in the poorest countries women often have eight children, the rate fell as low as 1.3 in some European countries such as Italy, which is below the replacement rate. Such a low rate has two likely negative consequences: the population will fall in the long term, and a growing number of old people will have to be supported by a shrinking number of young. But a recent study by researchers from Pennsylvania University suggests that this pattern may be changing. They related countries' fertility rates to their human development index (HDI), a figure with a maximum value of 1.0, which assesses life expectancy, average income and education level. Over 20 countries now have an HDI of more than 0.9, and in a majority of these the fertility rate has started to increase, and in some is approaching two children per woman. Although there are exceptions such as Japan, it appears that ever higher levels of wealth and education eventually translate into a desire for more children.

▶ See Unit 1.5 Finding key points and note-making

■ **Complete the notes of the key points below.**

(a) Falling levels of fertility have generally been found _____

_____

(b) In some, number of children born _____

_____

(c) Two results: smaller populations and _____

_____

(d) Recent research claims that _____

_____

(e) Comparison of HDI (human development index: _____
_____) with fertility found
that in most highly rated (+0.9) countries, _____
_____

■ **Join the notes together and expand them to make the final summary. Check that the meaning is clear and no important points have been left out. Find a suitable title.**

This summary is about 35 per cent of the original length, but it could be summarised further.

■ **Summarise the summary in no more than 20 words.**

5 Practice C

■ **Summarise the following text in about 50 words.**

| 5.1 | **THE LAST WORD IN LAVATORIES?** |

Toto is a leading Japanese manufacturer of bathroom ceramic ware, with annual worldwide sales of around $5 bn. One of its best-selling ranges is the Washlet lavatory, priced at up to $5,000 and used in most Japanese homes. This has features such as a heated seat, and can play a range of sounds. This type of toilet is successful in its home market since many flats are small and crowded, and bathrooms provide valued privacy. Now Toto hopes to increase its sales in Europe and America, where it faces a variety of difficulties. European countries tend to have their own rules about lavatory design, so that different models have to be made for each market. Although Toto claims that its Washlet toilet uses less water than the average model, one factor that may delay its penetration into Europe is its need for an electrical socket for installation, as these are prohibited in bathrooms by most European building regulations.

References and quotations

Academic writing depends on the research and ideas of others, so it is vital to show which sources you have used in your work, in an acceptable manner. This unit explains:

- the format of in-text citation
- the main reference systems
- the use of quotations
- the layout of lists of references

---

1 Why use references?

There are three principal reasons for providing references and citations:

(a) To show that you have read some of the authorities on the subject, which will give added weight to your writing.

(b) To allow the reader to find the source, if he/ she wishes to examine the topic in more detail.

(c) To avoid plagiarism.

▶ **See Unit 1.3 Avoiding plagiarism**

■ **Decide if you need to give a reference in the following cases.**

	Y/N
(a) Data you found from your own primary research	
(b) A graph from an internet article	
(c) A quotation from a book	
(d) An item of common knowledge	
(e) A theory from a journal article	
(f) An idea of your own based on reading several sources	

2 Citations and references

It is important to refer correctly to the work of other writers that you have used. You may present these sources as either a summary/ paraphrase or as a quotation. In each case a citation is included to provide a link to the list of references at the end of your paper:

> Smith (2009) argues that the popularity of the Sports Utility Vehicle (SUV) is irrational, as despite their high cost most are never driven off-road. In his view 'they are bad for road safety, the environment and road congestion' (Smith, 2009: 37).

> **References**
>
> Smith, M. (2009) *Power and the State.* Basingstoke: Palgrave MacMillan.

■ **Underline the citations in the example above. Which is a summary and which a quotation? What are the advantages of each?**

Giving citations

A quotation	Author's name, date of publication, page no.	(Smith, 2009: 37)
A summary	Author's name, date of publication	Smith (2009)

3 Reference verbs

Summaries and quotations are usually introduced by a reference verb:

Smith (2009) **argues** that . . .

Janovic (1972) **claimed** that . . .

These verbs can be either in the present or the past tense. Normally the use of the present tense suggests that the source is recent and still valid, while the past indicates that the source is older and may be out-of-date, but there are no hard-and-fast distinctions. In some disciplines an old source may still have validity.

▶ **See Unit 3.14 Verbs of reference**

4 Reference systems

There are various systems of referencing in use in the academic world, so you should ask your teachers if you are not sure which to use. With any system, the most important point is to be consistent.

(a) The Harvard system, generally used for English Language and Business, illustrated in (2) above.

(b) The Vancouver system, widely used in Medicine and Science. Numbers in brackets are inserted after the citation and these link to a numbered list of references:

Jasanoff (5) makes the point that the risk of cross-infection is growing.

> (5) Jasanoff, M. *Tuberculosis: A Sub-Saharan Perspective.* New York: Schaffter (2001)

(c) The footnote system (also known as endnotes), commonly used in the Humanities, in which sources are listed at the bottom of the page and again at the end of the paper. The numbers in superscript run consecutively throughout the paper:

The effects of the French Revolution were felt throughout Europe.[3]

> 3   Karl Wildavsky, *The End of an Era: Spain 1785–1815*
>   (Dublin: University Press, 2006), p. 69

NB. Referencing is a complex subject and students should use an online reference guide for detailed information. Their university library may provide one.

For a full guide to the use of the Harvard system see:
   www.home.ched.coventry.ac.uk/caw/harvard/

For the Vancouver system see:
   www.imperial.ac.uk/Library/pdf/Vancouver_referencing.pdf

For the footnotes system see:
   www.resources.glos.ac.uk/shareddata/dms/9F4295CDBCD42
   A0399BA0A2A6E688835.pdf

5 Using quotations

Using a quotation means bringing the original words of a writer into your work. Quotations are effective in some situations, but must not be over-used. They can be valuable:

*   when the original words express an idea in a distinctive way

*   when the original is more concise than your summary could be

*   when the original version is well-known

All quotations should be introduced by a phrase that shows the source, and also explains how this quotation fits into your argument:

Introductory phrase	Author	Reference verb	Quotation	Citation
This view is widely shared;	as Friedman	stated:	'Inflation is the one form of taxation that can be imposed without legislation'	(1974: 93).

(a) Short quotations (2–3 lines) are shown by single quotation marks. Quotations inside quotations (nested quotations) use double:

> As James remarked: 'Martin's concept of "internal space" requires close analysis.'

(b) Longer quotations are either indented (given a wider margin) or are printed in smaller type. In this case quotations marks are not needed.

(c) Page numbers should be given after the date.

(d) Care must be taken to ensure that quotations are the exact words of the original. If it is necessary to delete some words that are irrelevant, use points . . . to show where the missing section was:

> 'Few inventions . . . have been as significant as the mobile phone.'

(e) It may be necessary to insert a word or phrase into the quotation to clarify a point. This can be done by using square brackets [ ]:

> 'modern ideas [of freedom] differ radically from those of the ancient world. . .'

6 Practice

■ Study the following paragraph from an article titled 'The mobile revolution' in the journal 'Development Quarterly' (Issue 34 pages 85–97, 2009) by K. Hoffman. p. 87.

6.1a According to recent estimates there are at least 4 billion mobile phones in the world, and the majority of these are owned by people in the developing world. Ownership in the developed world reached saturation level by 2007, so countries such as China, India and Brazil now account for most of the growth. In the poorest countries, with weak transport networks and unreliable postal services, access to telecommunications is a vital tool for starting or developing a business, since it provides access to wider markets. Studies have shown that when household incomes rise, more money is spent on mobile phones than any other item.

(a) **Summary**

Hoffman (2009) stresses the critical importance of mobile phones in the developing world in the growth of small businesses.

(b) **Quotation**

According to Hoffman, mobile phone ownership compensates for the weaknesses of infrastructure in the developing world: 'In the poorest countries, with weak transport networks and unreliable postal services, access to telecommunications is a vital tool for starting or developing a business, since it provides access to wider markets' (2009: 87).

(c) **Summary and quotation**

Hoffman points out that most of the growth in mobile phone ownership now takes place in the developing world, where it has become crucial for establishing a business: '. . . access to telecommunications is a vital tool for starting or developing a business, since it provides access to wider markets' (2009: 87).

■ **Read the next paragraph of the same article, also on p. 87.**

6.1b   In such countries the effect of phone ownership on GDP growth is much stronger than in the developed world, because the ability to make calls is being offered for the first time, rather than as an alternative to existing landlines. As a result, mobile phone operators have emerged in Africa, India and other parts of Asia that are larger and more flexible than Western companies, and which have grown by catering for poorer customers, being therefore well-placed to expand downmarket. In addition Chinese phone makers have successfully challenged the established Western companies in terms of quality as well as innovation. A further trend is the provision of services via the mobile network which offer access to information about topics such as healthcare or agriculture.

■ (a) Write a summary of the main point, including a citation.

■ (b) Introduce a quotation to show the key point, referring to the source.

■ (c) Combine (a) and (b), again acknowledging the source.

@ Referencing>

7 Abbreviations in citations

In-text citations use the following abbreviations, derived from Latin and printed in italics:

> *et al.*: normally used when there are three or more authors. The full list of names is given in the reference list:

> Many Americans fail to vote (Hobolt *et al.*, 2006: 137).

> *ibid.*: taken from the same source (i.e. the same page) as the previous citation:

> Older Americans are more likely to vote than the young *(ibid.)* . . .

> *op. cit.*: taken from the same source as previously, but a different page.

8 Organising the list of references

At the end of an essay or report there must be a list of all the sources cited in the writing.

In the Harvard system, illustrated here, the list is organised alphabetically by the family name of the author. You should be clear about the difference between first names and family names. On title pages the normal format of first name then family name is used:

> Sheila Burford, Juan Gonzalez

But in citations only the family name is used:

> Burford (2001), Gonzalez (1997)

In reference lists use the family name and the initial(s):

> Burford, S., Gonzalez, J.

If you are not sure which name is the family name, ask a classmate from that cultural background.

■ Study the reference list below, from an essay on the effects of age on second language learning, and answer the following questions.

8.1 REFERENCES

Bialystock, E. (1997) 'The structure of age: In search of barriers to second language acquisition'. *Second Language Research* 13 (2) 116-37.

Dörnyei, Z. (2009) *The Psychology of Second Language Acquisition*. Oxford: Oxford University Press.

Flege, J. (1999) 'Age of learning and second language speech' in Birdsong, D. (ed.) *Second Language Acquisition and the Critical Period Hypothesis*. London: Lawrence Erlbaum Associates 101-32.

Gass, S. and Selinker, L. (2001) *Second Language Acquisition: An Introductory Course*. London: Lawrence Erlbaum Associates.

Larson-Hall, J. (2008) 'Weighing the benefits of studying a foreign language at a younger starting age in a minimal input situation'. *Second Language Research* 24 (1) 35-63.

Myles, F. (nd) 'Second language acquisition (SLA) research: its significance for learning and teaching issues'. Subject Centre for Languages, Linguistics and Area Studies. www.llas.ac.uk/resources/gpg/421. Accessed 1 May 2010.

The International Commission on Second Language Acquisition (nd) 'What is SLA?' http://hw.ac.uk/langWWW/icsla/icsla.htm#SLA. Accessed 6 May 2010.

(a) Find an example of:

  (i)   a book by one author

  (ii) a journal article

  (iii) a chapter in an edited book

  (iv) an authored undated website article

  (v)   an anonymous webpage

  (vi) a book by two authors

(b) What are the main differences in the way these sources are
    referenced?

    (i) _____

    (ii) _____

    (iii) _____

    (iv) _____

    (v) _____

    (vi) _____

(c) When are italics used?

(d) How are capital letters used in titles?

(e) How is a source with no given author listed?

(f) Write citations for summaries from each of the sources.

    (i) _____

    (ii) _____

    (iii) _____

    (iv) _____

    (v) _____

    (vi) _____

    (vii) _____

Combining sources

For most assignments students are expected to read a variety of sources, often reflecting conflicting views on a topic. In some cases the contrast between the various views may be the focus of the task. This unit explains how a writer can present and organise a range of contrasting sources.

1 Mentioning sources

In the early stages of an essay it is common to mention the contributions of other writers to the subject, to show that you are familiar with their work.

■ **Read the following example, from a comparison of 'technology readiness' in Chinese and American consumers, and answer the questions below.**

(a) How many sources are mentioned here?

(b) What was the subject of Meuter, Ostrom, Bitner and Roundtree's research?

(c) Which source contrasted fear of computers with playing with computers?

(d) Which source examined the paradox of positive and negative attitudes to computers?

(e) How many sources are cited that studied attitudes to particular technologies?

> **1.1**   The extent to which consumers desire to use new technology is
>   commonly influenced by factors such as consumer attitudes toward
> specific technologies (Bobbit and Dabholkar, 2001; Curran *et al.*, 2003), the level
> of technology anxiety exhibited by consumers (Meuter, Ostrom, Bitner and
> Roundtree, 2003), and consumer capacity and willingness (Walker, Lees, Hecker
> and Francis, 2002). Mick and Fournier (1998) argue that consumers can
> simultaneously exhibit positive feelings (such as intelligence and efficacy) and
> negative feelings (such as ignorance and ineptitude) towards new technology.
> Venkatesh (2000) found that 'computer playfulness' and 'computer anxiety' serve
> as anchors that users employ in forming perceptions of ease of use about new
> technology.

▶ **See Unit 4.3 Reports, case studies and literature reviews**

2 Taking a critical approach

■ The two texts below reflect different views on the topic of climate
change. Read them both and then study the extract from an essay that
mentions the two sources. Answer the questions that follow.

> **2.1a**   **CLIMATE CHANGE**
>
> Most scientists now agree that global temperatures have risen over the last
> century, and that this trend is reflected in such phenomena as the melting of sea
> ice and the retreat of glaciers. There is also a consensus that over the period the
> level of carbon dioxide (CO_2) in the earth's atmosphere has also risen, mainly as
> a result of burning fossil fuels such as coal and oil. The common view is that the
> first change is the result of the second; in other words a warmer climate has been
> caused by the CO_2, which has the effect of causing the warmth from the sun's
> rays to be trapped inside the atmosphere; the so-called 'greenhouse effect'. If
> these theories are accepted it can be expected that temperatures will continue to
> increase in future as carbon dioxide levels rise, and since this will have harmful
> effects on agriculture and other human activities, efforts should be made to
> reduce the burning of fossil fuels.
>
> (Lombardo, 2009)

2.1b   The conventional view that global warming is caused by a rise in carbon dioxide levels has been criticised on a number of grounds. Some critics claim that the recent period of warming is part of a natural cycle of temperature fluctuations which have been recorded over the past few thousand years. They point out that Europe experienced a warm period about 800 years ago which was unrelated to CO_2 levels. Other critics doubt the reliability of the basic temperature data and maintain that the apparent rise in temperatures is caused by the growth of cities, regarded as 'heat islands'. In addition some claim that the warming is caused by a reduction in cloud cover, allowing more sunlight to reach the earth's surface. This effect, they believe, is the result of solar activity or sunspots, which are known to fluctuate on an 11-year cycle. As a result of these doubts, sceptics argue that there is no need to attempt to reduce the industrial activity that causes carbon dioxide to be produced.

(Wong, 2007)

2.2   **HOW STRONG IS THE EVIDENCE FOR GLOBAL WARMING?**

Lombardo (2009) puts forward the view that the significant rise in the earth's temperature over the past century is the product of increased levels of atmospheric CO_2 caused by greater use of fossil fuels. He maintains that this position is now generally agreed, and that steps should be taken to reduce future warming by restricting the output of greenhouse gases such as carbon dioxide. However, Wong (2007) presents a range of counter-arguments. She mentions evidence of historical climate change which cannot have been caused by rising levels of CO_2, and also discusses the difficulty of obtaining reliable data on temperature changes, as well as other claims that solar activity may affect the amount of cloud cover and hence temperature levels. Such uncertainty, she considers, may raise doubts about the value of cutting CO_2 production.

■ (a) The extract above summarises ideas from both Lombardo and
   Wong. Find two examples of a summary in the extract and match them
   with the original text from (a) or (b).

Summary	Original
Example: ... the significant rise in the earth's temperature over the past century is the product of increased levels of atmospheric CO2 caused by greater use of fossil fuels.	There is also a consensus that over the period the level of carbon dioxide (CO_2) in the earth's atmosphere has also risen, mainly as a result of burning fossil fuels such as coal and oil.

(b) Which verbs are used to introduce the summaries?

_____

(c) Which word marks the point where the writer switches from
    summarising Lombardo to Wong?

_____

(d) What other words or phrases could be used at this point?

_____

3 Combining three sources

■ Read the third text on climate change below, and then complete the
paragraph from the essay above titled:

'How strong is the evidence for global warming?'

by summarising Lahav's comments.

3.1   Debate on the issues around climate change have intensified recently,
since while most scientists agree that global temperatures are rising as
a result of ever-higher levels of carbon dioxide in the earth's atmosphere, a
minority continue to argue that the rise is insignificant, short term or unrelated
to CO_2 levels. The controversy clearly has important political and economic
consequences, since international agreement is needed to control the output of
greenhouse gases. Climate sceptics insist that computer models are unable to
handle the complexity of the world's weather systems, and so should not be used
as a basis for making major decisions. Their view is that because the science of
global warming is uncertain, the money that would be spent, for example, on
building wind farms could be better spent on improving health and education in
the developing world.

(Lahav, 2010)

@   Combining sources>

Organising paragraphs

Paragraphs are the basic building blocks of academic writing. Well-structured paragraphs help the reader understand the topic more easily by dividing up the argument into convenient sections. This unit looks at:

- the components of paragraphs
- the way the components are linked together
- the linkage between paragraphs in the overall text

1 Paragraph structure

■ **Discuss the following questions.**

- What is a paragraph?
- What is the normal length of a paragraph?
- Is there a standard structure for paragraphs?
- How is a paragraph linked together?

2 Example paragraph

■ Study the paragraph below. It is from the introduction to an essay titled

'Should home ownership be encouraged?'

> **2.1**   The rate of home ownership varies widely across the developed world. Germany, for instance, has one of the lowest rates, at 42 per cent, while in Spain it is twice as high, 85 per cent. Both the USA and Britain have similar rates of about 69 per cent. The reasons for this variation appear to be more cultural and historic than economic, since high rates are found in both rich and poorer countries. There appears to be no conclusive link between national prosperity and the number of homeowners.

This paragraph can be analysed:

1 Topic sentence	The rate of home ownership varies widely across the developed world.
2 Example 1	Germany, **for instance**, has one of the lowest rates, at 42 per cent, **while** in Spain it is twice as high, 85 per cent.
3 Example 2	Both the USA and Britain have similar rates of about 69 per cent.
4 Reason	**The reasons for** this variation appear to be more cultural and historic than economic, **since** high rates are found in both rich and poorer countries.
5 Summary	**There appears to be** no conclusive link between national prosperity and the number of homeowners.

This example shows that:

(a) A paragraph is a group of sentences that deal with a single topic.

(b) The length of paragraphs varies significantly according to text type, but should be no less than four or five sentences.

(c) Normally (but not always) the first sentence introduces the topic. Other sentences may give definitions, examples, information, reasons, restatements and summaries.

(d) The parts of the paragraph are linked together by the phrases and conjunctions shown in bold in the table. They guide the reader through the arguments presented.

3 Practice A

■ **Read the next paragraph from the same essay and answer the questions below.**

> **3.1** Despite this, many countries encourage the growth of home ownership. Ireland and Spain, for example, allow mortgage payers to offset payments against income tax. It is widely believed that owning your own home has social as well as economic benefits. Compared to renters, homeowners are thought to be more stable members of the community who contribute more to local affairs. In addition, neighbourhoods of owner occupiers are considered to have less crime and better schools. But above all, ownership encourages saving and allows families to build wealth.

(a) Analyse the paragraph by completing the left hand column in the table below with the following types of sentence:
Supporting point 1, Supporting point 2, Supporting point 3, Example, Reason, Topic.

	Despite this, many countries encourage the growth of home ownership.
	Ireland and Spain, for example, allow mortgage payers to offset payments against income tax.
	It is widely believed that owning your own home has social as well as economic benefits.
Supporting point 1	Compared to renters, homeowners are thought to be more stable members of the community who contribute more to local affairs.
	In addition, neighbourhoods of owner occupiers are considered to have less crime and better schools.
	But above all, ownership encourages saving and allows families to build wealth.

(b) Underline the words and phrases used to link the sentences together.

(c) Which phrase is used to link this paragraph to the one before?

4 Development of ideas

■ (a) The sentences below form the third paragraph of the same essay, but they have been mixed up. Use the table below to put them in the correct order.

(i) These had been developed to allow higher-risk poorer families to buy their own homes, but contributed to a property price bubble.

(ii) Many economists now argue that there is a maximum level of home ownership that should not be exceeded.

(iii) All these claims were challenged by the economic crash of 2008, which was in large part caused by defaults on American sub-prime mortgages.

(iv) Even households that had positive equity still felt poorer and reduced their spending.

(v) Others were trapped in their houses by negative equity, in other words their houses were worth less than they had paid for them.

(vi) When this burst, millions of people lost their homes, which for many had contained their savings.

Topic sentence	All these claims were challenged by the economic crash of 2008, which was in large part caused by defaults on American sub-prime mortgages.
Definition	
Result 1	
Result 2	
Result 3	
Conclusion	

(b) Underline the phrase used to link the paragraph to the previous one.

(c) Underline the words and phrases used to link the paragraph together.

5 Linking paragraphs together

In the examples above, each new paragraph begins with a phrase that links it to the previous paragraph, in order to maintain continuity of argument:

> *Despite this* (i.e. the lack of a conclusive link)
> *All these claims* (i.e. arguments in favour of home ownership)

In order to begin a new topic you may use:

> *Turning to the issue of . . .*
> *Rates of infection must also be examined . . .*
> *. . . is another area for consideration*

Paragraphs can also be introduced with adverbs:

> *Traditionally, few examples were . . .*
> *Finally, the performance of . . .*

6 Practice B

■ (a) Use the notes below and the table on p. 82 to complete a paragraph of an essay titled:

'High rates of home ownership are bad for the economy – Discuss.'

- It is claimed that increases in rate of home ownership lead to unemployment

- Home ownership appears to make people more reluctant to move to find work

- e.g. Spain (high ownership + high unemployment) vs. Switzerland (low ownership + low unemployment)

- Other factors have been proposed, e.g. liquidity of housing markets (how easy to sell houses)

- Theory still controversial

1 **Topic**	*It has been argued that rises in the rate of home ownership can increase the rate of unemployment.*
2 **Reason**	
3 **Example**	
4 **Argument**	
5 **Conclusion**	

■ (b) Use the notes below to write the next paragraph of the essay, including a phrase linking it to the previous paragraph.

- Recession of 2008–9 gave support to theory in some US states (e.g. California, Michigan and Florida)
- They had major housing boom in 1990s
- After recession rate of house moving fell sharply
- One factor was number of households in negative equity
- Having negative equity means selling house at loss
- High rates of ownership may deepen recession if labour is more static

1	
2	
3	
4	
5	
6	

Introductions and conclusions

An effective introduction explains the purpose and scope of the paper to the reader. The conclusion should provide a clear answer to any question asked in the title, as well as summarising the main points. In coursework both introductions and conclusions are normally written after the main body.

1 Introduction contents

Introductions are usually no more than about 10 per cent of the total length of the assignment. Therefore in a 2,000 word essay the introduction would be about 200 words.

■ **(a) What is normally found in an essay introduction? Choose from the list below.**

		Y/N
(i)	A definition of any unfamiliar terms in the title.	
(ii)	Your opinions on the subject of the essay.	
(iii)	Mention of some sources you have read on the topic.	
(iv)	A provocative idea or question to interest the reader.	
(v)	Your aim or purpose in writing.	
(vi)	The method you adopt to answer the question (or an outline).	
(vii)	Some brief background to the topic.	
(viii)	Any limitations you set yourself.	

■ **(b) Read the extracts below from introductions to articles and decide which of the functions listed above (i – viii) they are examples of.**

(i)   In the past 20 years the ability of juries to assess complex or lengthy cases has been widely debated.

(ii) The rest of the paper is organised as follows. The second section explains why corporate governance is important for economic prosperity. The third section presents the model specification and describes the data and variables used in our empirical analysis. The fourth section reports and discusses the empirical results. The fifth section concludes.

(iii) The purpose of this paper is to investigate changes in the incidence of extreme warm and cold temperatures over the globe since 1870.

(iv) There is no clear empirical evidence sustaining a 'managerial myopia' argument. Pugh *et al.* (1992) find evidence that supports such theory, but Meulbrook *et al.* (1990), Mahoney *et al.* (1997), Garvey and Hanka (1999) and a study by the Office of the Chief Economist of the Securities and Exchange Commission (1985) find no evidence.

(v)   'Social cohesion' is usually defined in reference to common aims and objectives, social order, social solidarity and the sense of place attachment.

(vi) This study will focus on mergers in the media business between 1990 and 2005, since with more recent examples an accurate assessment of the consequences cannot yet be made.

2 Introduction structure

Not every introduction will include all the elements listed above.

■ **Which are essential and which are optional?**

There is no standard pattern for an introduction, since much depends on the type of research you are conducting and the length of your work, but a common framework is:

a	Definition of key terms, if needed.
b	Relevant background information.
c	Review of work by other writers on the topic.
d	Purpose or aim of the paper.
e	Your methods and the results you found.
f	Any limitations you imposed.
g	The organisation of your work.

■ **Study the extracts below from the introduction to an essay titled:**

'Evaluate the experience of e-learning for students in higher education.'

(a) Certain words or phrases in the title may need clarifying because they are not widely understood:

There are a range of definitions of this term, but in this paper 'e-learning' refers to any type of learning situation where content is delivered via the internet.

▶ **See Unit 2.5 Definitions**

(b) It is useful to remind the reader of the wider context of your work. This may also show the value of the study you have carried out:

Learning is one of the most vital components of the contemporary knowledge-based economy. With the development of computing power and technology the internet has become an essential medium for knowledge transfer.

(c) While a longer article may have a separate literature review, in a shorter essay it is still important to show familiarity with researchers who have studied this topic previously. This may also reveal a gap in research that justifies your work:

Various researchers (Webb and Kirstin, 2003; Honig *et al.*, 2006) have evaluated e-learning in a healthcare and business context, but little attention so far has been paid to the reactions of students in higher education to this method of teaching.

(d) The aim of your research must be clearly stated so the reader knows what you are trying to do:

> The purpose of this study was to examine students' experience of e-learning in a higher education context.

(e) The method demonstrates the process that you undertook to achieve the aim given before:

> A range of studies was first reviewed, and then a survey of 200 students from a variety of disciplines was conducted to assess their experience of e-learning.

(f) You cannot deal with every aspect of this topic in an essay, so you must make clear the boundaries of your study:

> Clearly a study of this type is inevitably restricted by various constraints, notably the size of the student sample, and this was limited to students of Pharmacy and Agriculture.

(g) Understanding the structure of your work will help the reader to follow your argument:

> The paper is structured as follows. The first section presents an analysis of the relevant research, focusing on the current limited knowledge regarding the student experience. The second part . . .

3 Opening sentences

It can be difficult to start writing an essay, but especially in exams, hesitation will waste valuable time. The first few sentences should be general but not vague, to help the reader focus on the topic. They often have the following pattern:

Time phrase	Topic	Development
Currently,	the control of water resources	has emerged as potential cause of international friction.
Since 2008	electric vehicles	have become a serious commercial proposition.

It is important to avoid opening sentences that are over-general. Compare:

> Nowadays there is a lot of competition among different providers of news.

> Newspapers are currently facing strong competition from rival news providers such as the internet and television.

■ **Write introductory sentences for three of the following titles.**

(a) How important is it for companies to have women as senior managers?

_____

(b) Are there any technological solutions to global warming?

_____

(c) What can be done to reduce infant mortality in developing countries?

_____

(d) Compare the urbanisation process in two contrasting countries.

_____

▶ See Unit 2.7 Generalisations

4 Practice A

■ **You have to write an essay with the title**

'Can everyone benefit from higher education?'

■ **Use the notes below to write the introduction in about 150 words (it is not necessary to refer to sources in this exercise).**

Definition: Higher education (HE) = university education

Background: Increasing demand for HE worldwide puts pressure on national budgets > many states seek to shift costs to students. In most countries degree = key to better jobs and opportunities

Purpose: To decide if access to HE should be restricted or open to all, given costs involved

Method/Outline: Discussion of following points:

   HE is expensive, so who will pay?

   Increasing numbers = lower quality

   Is it fair for all taxpayers to support students who will earn
   high salaries?

   How to keep HE open to clever students from poor backgrounds?

Limitations: The use of your own country as an example

5 Conclusions

Conclusions tend to be shorter and more diverse than introductions. Some
articles may have a 'summary' or 'concluding remarks'. But student papers
should generally have a final section that summarises the arguments and
makes it clear to the reader that the original question has been answered.

■ **Which of the following are generally acceptable in conclusions?**

(a) A statement showing how your aim has been achieved.

(b) A discussion of the implications of your research.

(c) Some new information on the topic not mentioned before.

(d) A short review of the main points of your study.

(e) Some suggestions for further research.

(f) The limitations of your study.

(g) Comparison with the results of similar studies.

(h) A quotation that appears to sum up your work.

■ **Match the extracts from conclusions below with the acceptable components above.**

Example: a = vi

(i)   As always, this investigation has a number of limitations to be considered in evaluating its findings.

(ii) These results suggest that the risk of flooding on this coast has increased significantly and is likely to worsen.

(iii) Another line of research worth pursuing further is to study the importance of language for successful expatriate assignments.

(iv) Our review of 13 studies of strikes in public transport demonstrates that the effect of a strike on public transport ridership varies and may either be temporary or permanent.

(v)   These results of the Colombia study reported here are consistent with other similar studies conducted in other countries (Baron and Norman, 1992).

(vi) This study has clearly illustrated the drawbacks to family ownership of retail businesses.

6 Practice B

■ **Look at Unit 1.10 Organising paragraphs, section 6. Study the notes for the first two paragraphs, then write a concluding paragraph that summarises the main points and answers the question in the title (i.e. Are high rates of home ownership bad for the economy?). Discuss any implications that arise and suggest possible further research.**

Re-writing and proof-reading

> In exams you have no time for re-writing, but for coursework assignments it is important to take time to revise your work to improve its clarity and logical development. In both situations proof-reading is essential to avoid the small errors that may make parts of your work inaccurate or even incomprehensible.

1 Re-writing

Although it is tempting to think that the first draft of an essay is adequate, it is almost certain that it can be improved. After completing your first draft you should leave it for a day and then re-read it, asking the following questions:

(a) Does this fully answer the question(s) in the title?

(b) Do the different sections of the paper have the right weight, i.e. is it well balanced?

(c) Does the argument or discussion develop clearly and logically?

(d) Have I forgotten any important points that would support the development?

2 Practice A

■ As part of a module on Qualitative Research Methods, you have written the first draft of a 1,000 word paper titled: 'What would be an acceptable number of interviews to carry out for a Master's dissertation?'

■ Study the introduction to this paper below, and decide how it could be improved, listing your suggestions in the table.

2.1   An interview can be defined as a conversation with a definite structure and objective. It goes beyond an everyday discussion with no particular purpose. There are many possible interview situations, but all involve an interviewer and an interviewee. It is normal for the former to ask the latter direct questions, and record the answers. The questions may be prepared in advance or they may occur as the interview develops. The recording is often done on paper, but may also be done by audio or video recording. Interviews can take place anywhere, in a street, café, office, bar, restaurant etc. It is hard to say how many interviews can be carried out in one day. I personally think that two is the maximum because it can get very tiring. A lot depends on the subject being researched.

Suggestions for improvement
(a)
(b)
(c)
(d)
(e)

Comments on the first draft might include some of the following:

a) Too much space given to basic points
b) No references are given
c) Sentences are too short
d) Style e.g. *I personally think* not suitable
e) Question in title not addressed

With these points in mind, the introduction could be re-written as follows:

2.2   Organising an interview involves a series of steps (Davies, 2007) including recruiting interviewees, finding a suitable venue and writing appropriate guidelines. However, depending on the research subject a more flexible approach can be adopted, resulting in a less structured interview (Cooper and Schindler, 2008). For a Master's dissertation, interviews must contain data relevant to the research topic which the interviewer can later process. As King states: 'gathering a large volume of cases does not guarantee the credibility of a study' (King, 2004: 16). Most writers agree that two one-hour interviews per day are effectively the maximum for one interviewer, given the time needed for preparation and subsequent processing. Moreover, if audio or video recording is used there is more content to be analysed, for instance in terms of facial expression. The analysis of one interview can take up to three days' work. In order to answer the question, clearly much depends on the research topic and the time the researcher has available.

3 Practice B

■ **Read the next section on 'Possible ethical issues raised by this kind of research'.**

■ **Decide how it could be improved, and re-write it in the box below.**

> **3.1** Any organisation that allows researchers to interview its employees runs a risk. They may complain about the boss or about other workers. The danger is that employees may feel obliged to give positive answers to questions instead of their honest opinions, because they are afraid of their bosses finding out what they really think. The reputation of the organisation may suffer. So it is the duty of researchers to ensure that this does not happen. They must make it clear why they are doing the research, and maintain the anonymity of everyone involved by using false names. If this is not done there is a good chance of the validity of the whole research project being threatened.

4 Proof-reading

(a) Proof-reading means checking your work for small errors that may make it more difficult for the reader to understand exactly what you want to say. If a sentence has only one error:

She has no enough interpersonal skills to handle different relationships . . .

it is not difficult to understand, but if there are multiple errors, even though they are all quite minor, the cumulative effect is very confusing:

Demolition of sevral uk banks like northren Rock and may others . . .

Clearly, you should aim to make your meaning as clear as possible. Note that computer spellchecks do not always help you, since they may ignore a word that is spelt correctly but that is not the word you meant to use:

Tow factors need to be considered . . .

■ **(b) Examples of the most common types of error in student writing are shown below. In each case underline the error and correct it.**

(i)   Factual: *corruption is a problem in many countries such as Africa*

(ii)   Word ending: *she was young and innocence*

(iii)   Punctuation: *However some strains of malaria are resistant . . .*

(iv)   Tense: *Since 2005 there were three major earthquakes in the region*

(v)   Vocabulary: *. . . vital to the successfulness of a company operating in China*

(vi)   Spelling: *pervious experience can sometimes give researchers . . .*

(vii)   Singular/plural: *one of the largest company in Asia*

(viii) Style: *. . . finally, the essay will conclude with a conclusion*

(ix)   Missing word: *an idea established by David Ricardo in nineteenth century*

(x)   Word order: *a rule of marketing which states that consumers when go out shopping . . .*

■ **(c) The following extracts each contain one type of error. Match each to one of the examples (i–x) above, and correct the error.**

(i)   Products like Tiger biscuits are well-known to kids . . .

(ii)   Both companies focus on mass marketing to promote its line of products.

(iii)   Failure to find the right coffee may lead to torment for consumers.

(iv)   . . . different researchers have differently effects on the research.

(v)   After the single European market was established in 1873 . . .

(vi)   . . . experienced researchers can most likely come over these problems.

(vii) Firstly because, it provides them with an opportunity of borrowing capital . . .

(viii) The company selected Hungry for setting up its research centre.

(ix)   These cases demonstrate why specialists from the rest of world are eager to . . .

(x)   Since 2003, few companies entered the French market . . .

■ **(d) Underline the errors in the paragraph below and then re-write it.**

4.1   **OPPORTUNITIES FOR NON-EUROPEAN BUSINESSES IN EUROPE**

Many non-European businesses are aiming to enter single European market as they see an unexploited potential there. There are two reasons of this interest. Firstly the non-european organisations are keen to do a business in the European markets because it is one of leading investment destination and easiest place to set up and run a business. Secondly, the single European market provide forein investors with an internationally competitive tax environment. Lastly there's lots of rich people living in the country.

@   Proof-reading>

5 Confusing pairs

When proof-reading it is important to check for mistakes with some confusing pairs of words, which have similar but distinct spellings and meanings:

> The drought **affected** the wheat harvest in Australia.

> An immediate **effect** of the price rise was a fall in demand.

'Affect' and 'effect' are two different words. 'Affect' is a verb, while 'effect' is commonly used as a noun.

■ **Study the differences between other similar confusing pairs (most common uses in brackets).**

accept (verb)/ except (prep)
    It is difficult to **accept** their findings.
    The report is finished **except** for the conclusion.

compliment (noun/ verb)/ complement (verb)
    Her colleagues **complimented** her on her presentation.
    His latest book **complements** his previous research on African politics.

economic (adj)/ economical (adj)
    Sharing a car to work was an **economical** move.
    Inflation was one **economic** result of the war.

its (pronoun)/ it's (pronoun + verb)
    It's widely agreed that carbon emissions are rising.
    The car's advanced design was **its** most distinct feature.

lose (verb)/ loose (adj)
    No general ever plans to **lose** a battle.
    He stressed the **loose** connection between religion and psychology.

principal (adj/ noun)/ principle (noun)
    All economists recognise the **principle** of supply and demand.
    Zurich is the **principal** city of Switzerland.

rise (verb – past tense rose)/ raise (verb – past tense raised)
    The population of Sydney **rose** by 35% in the century.
    The university **raised** its fees by 10% last year.

---

site (noun)/ sight (noun)
> The **site** of the battle is now covered by an airport.
> His **sight** began to weaken when he was in his eighties.

tend to (verb)/ trend (noun)
> Young children **tend** to enjoy making a noise.
> In many countries there is a **trend** towards smaller families.

■ Choose the correct word in each sentence.

(a) The company was founded on the <u>principals/ principles</u> of quality and value.

(b) Millions of people are attempting to <u>lose/ loose</u> weight.

(c) Sunspots have been known to <u>affect/ effect</u> radio communication.

(d) Professor Poledna received their <u>compliments/ complements</u> politely.

(e) The ancient symbol depicted a snake eating <u>it's/ its</u> tail.

(f) Both social and <u>economical/ economic</u> criteria need to be examined.

(g) It took many years for some of Einstein's theories to be <u>accepted/ excepted</u>.

Elements of writing

Argument and discussion

On most courses it is not enough to show that you are familiar with the leading authorities. Students are expected to study the conflicting views on any topic and engage with them. This means analysing and critiquing them if appropriate. This unit presents ways of demonstrating your familiarity with both sides of an argument and presenting your own conclusions in a suitably academic manner.

1 Discussion vocabulary

Essay titles commonly ask students to 'discuss' a topic:

'Children will learn a foreign language more easily if it is integrated with another subject – Discuss.'

This requires an evaluation of both the benefits and disadvantages of the topic, with a section of the essay, sometimes headed 'Discussion', in which a summary of these is made. The following vocabulary can be used:

+	−
benefit advantage a positive aspect pro (informal) plus (informal) one major advantage is . . .	drawback disadvantage a negative feature con (informal) minus (informal) a serious drawback is . . .

*One **drawback** to integrating content and language is the demand it places on the teacher.*

*A **significant** benefit of teaching a subject through a language is the increased motivation to master the language.*

■ **Fill the gaps in the following paragraph using language from the table above.**

Every year millions of students choose to study in a foreign country. This can have considerable (a)_____, such as the chance to experience another culture, but also involves certain (b)_____, which may include feelings of isolation or homesickness. Another (c)_____ aspect may be the high cost, involving both fees and living expenses. However, most students appear to find that the (d)_____ outweigh the (e) _____, and that the chance to join an international group of students is a major (f)_____ in developing a career.

2 Organisation

The discussion section can be organised in two ways; either by grouping the benefits in one paragraph and the disadvantages in another (vertical), or by examining the subject from different viewpoints (horizontal). For example, the following essay title can be discussed in the two ways as shown:

'Prisons do little to reform criminals and their use should be limited – Discuss.'

(a) Vertical

Drawbacks: Prisons are expensive, may be 'universities of crime', most prisoners re-offend after leaving, many prisoners have mental health problems that are untreated.
Benefits: Prisons isolate dangerous criminals from society, act as a deterrent to criminal activity, may provide education or treatment (e.g. for drug addiction), provide punishment for wrong-doing.
Discussion: Numbers of prisoners are rising in many countries, which suggests that the system is failing. Evidence that short sentences are of little value. But prisons will always be necessary for some violent criminals, and as deterrent.

(b) Horizontal

Economic: High costs of keeping prisoners secure. Compare with other forms of punishment.
Ethical: What rights should prisoners have? Cases of wrongful imprisonment.
Social: Effect on families of prisoners, especially female prisoners with children. But also necessary to consider the victims of crime, especially violent crime.
Discussion: Numbers of prisoners are rising in many countries, which suggests that the system is failing. Evidence that short sentences are of little value. But prisons will always be necessary for some violent criminals, and as deterrent.

■ **What are the advantages of each format (i.e. vertical and horizontal)?**

3 Practice A

You have to write an essay titled:

'Discuss whether some employees should be permitted to work from home.'

■ **Brainstorm the positive and negative aspects in the box below, and then write an outline using one of the structures (vertical or horizontal) above.**

+	−
No time spent commuting to work	

Discuss whether some employees should be permitted to work from home.

Outline

-
-
-
-
-
-
-

4 The language of discussion

When discussing common ideas avoid personal phrases such as *in my opinion* or *personally, I think* . . .

Use impersonal phrases instead such as:

It is generally accepted that	working from home saves commuting time . . .
It is widely agreed that	email and the internet reduce reliance on an office . . .
Most people appear	to need face-to-face contact with colleagues . . .
It is probable that	more companies will encourage working from home . . .
The evidence suggests that	certain people are better at self-management . . .

These phrases suggest a minority viewpoint:

It can be argued that	home-working encourages time-wasting
One view is that	home-workers become isolated

When you are supporting your opinions with sources use phrases such as:

According to Emerson (2003)	few companies have developed clear policies . . .
Poledna (2007) claims that	most employees benefit from flexible arrangements

5 Counter-arguments

Counter-arguments are ideas that are opposite to your ideas. In an academic discussion you must show that you are familiar with both sides of the argument, and provide reasons to support your position. It is usual to deal with the counter-arguments first, before giving your view.

■ **What is the writer's position in the following example, on the topic of prisons (2 above)?**

> **5.1**   It is claimed that prisons are needed to isolate dangerous criminals from society, but while this may be true in some cases, more commonly prisons act as 'universities of crime', which reinforce criminal behaviour.

■ **Study the example below, and write two more sentences using ideas from the title in (3).**

Counter-argument	Your position
Some people believe that home-workers become isolated,	*but this can be avoided by holding weekly meetings for all departmental staff.*

6 Providing evidence

Normally your conclusions on a topic follow an assessment of the evidence. You must show that you have studied the relevant sources since only then can you give a balanced judgement.

■ **Study the following text, which discusses the idea that young people today, who have grown up with computing and the internet, are different from previous generations.**

6.1 DO 'DIGITAL NATIVES' EXIST?

Various writers have argued that people born in the last two decades of the twentieth century (1980–2000) and who have been using computers all their lives have different abilities and needs to other people. Palfrey and Gasser (2008) refer to them as the 'net generation' and argue that activities such as putting videos on You Tube are more natural for them than writing essays. Similarly Prensky (2001a) claims that the educational system needs to be revised to cater for the preferences of these 'digital natives'.

But other researchers doubt that these claims can apply to a whole generation. Bennett, Maton and Kervin (2008) argue that these young people comprise a whole range of abilities, and that many of them only have a limited understanding of digital tools. They insist that the so-called 'digital native' theory is a myth, and that it would be a mistake to re-organise the educational system to cater for their supposed requirements. Clearly there are some young people who are very proficient in online technologies, but taking a global perspective many still grow up and are educated in a traditional manner. Teaching methods are constantly being revised, but there is no clear evidence of a need to radically change them.

■ The table below shows the structure of the text, but the descriptors have been mixed up. Re-arrange them in the correct order.

1	Arguments against
2	Writer's viewpoint
3	Claims for 'digital natives'

7 Practice B

■ Write two paragraphs on the topic: 'Is the exploration of space worthwhile?' Use the ideas below and make your stance clear.

Pros
- Scientists need to collect information to understand universe
- Space engineering has produced many useful discoveries (e.g. satellite communication)
- Exploration promotes healthy co-operation between nations (e.g. space station)

(Source: Donnet-Kammel, 2005)

Cons
- Huge amounts of money are spent with little result
- Resources should be spent on urgent needs on earth (e.g. disease control)
- National space programmes are testing potential weapons (e.g. missiles)

(Source: Soroka, 2000)

▶ See Unit 2.9 Problems and solutions

Cause and effect

Academic work frequently involves demonstrating a link between a cause, such as a cold winter, and an effect, such as an increase in illness. This unit explains two methods of describing the link, with the focus either on the cause or on the effect.

1 The language of cause and effect

A writer may choose to put the emphasis on either the cause or the effect. In both cases, either a verb or a conjunction can be used to show the link.

(a) Focus on causes

With verbs		
The heavy rain	caused created led to resulted in produced	the flood
With conjunctions		
Because of Due to Owing to As a result of	**the heavy rain**	there was a flood

(b) Focus on effects

With verbs		
The flood	was caused by was produced by resulted from (note use of passives)	the heavy rain
With conjunctions		
There was **a flood**	due to because of as a result of	the heavy rain

Compare the following:

Because children **were vaccinated** diseases declined
(because + verb)

Because of the **vaccination** diseases declined
(because of + noun)

As/ since children **were vaccinated** diseases declined
(conjunction + verb)

Owing to/ due to the **vaccination** diseases declined
(conjunction + noun)

Conjunctions are commonly used with specific situations, while verbs tend to be used in general cases:

Printing money commonly **leads to** inflation
(general)

Due to July's hot weather demand for ice cream increased
(specific)

2 Practice A

■ Match the causes with their likely effects and write sentences linking them together.

Causes	Effects
Cold winter of 1995	more tourists arriving
Higher rates of literacy	a new government being formed
Constructing an airport	reduced infant mortality
Last year's national election	greater demand for secondary education
Installing speed cameras on main roads	**increased demand for electricity**
Opening a new hospital in 2006	a fall in the number of fatal accidents

(a) *Owing to the cold winter of 1995 there was increased demand for electricity.*

(b) _____

_____

(c) _____

_____

(d) _____

_____

(e) _____

_____

(f) _____

_____

3 Practice B

■ Complete the following sentences with likely effects.

(a) Increasing use of the internet for shopping _____

_____

(b) The violent storms last week _____

_____

(c) The new vaccine for TB _____

_____

(d) Building a high-speed railway line _____

_____

■ **Complete these sentences with possible causes.**

(e) The serious motorway accident _____

_____

(f) The war of 1856–8 _____

_____

(g) Earthquakes _____

_____

(h) The rising prison population _____

_____

4 Practice C

■ **Use conjunctions or verbs to complete the following paragraph.**

4.1 WHY WOMEN LIVE LONGER

Some British scientists now believe that women live longer than men
(a)_____ T cells, a vital part of the immune system that protects the
body from diseases. Previously, various theories have attempted to explain
longer female life expectancy. Biologists claimed that women lived longer
(b)_____ they need to bring up children. Others argued that men
take more risks, (c)_____ they die earlier. But a team from Imperial
College think that the difference may be (d)_____ women having
better immune systems. Having studied a group of men and women they found
that the body produces fewer T cells as it gets older, (e)_____ the
ageing process. However, they admit that this may not be the only factor, and
(f)_____ another research project may be conducted.

5 Practice D

■ (a) Study the flow chart below, which shows some of the possible effects of a higher oil price. Complete the paragraph describing this sequence.

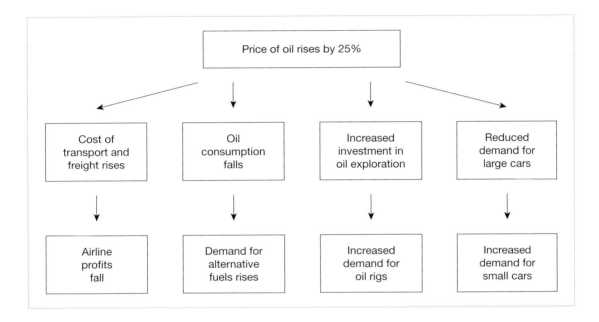

An increase of 25 per cent in the price of oil would have numerous results. First, it would lead to

■ (b) Choose a similar situation in your own subject. Draw a flow chart
showing some probable effects, and write a paragraph to describe
them.

Cohesion

Cohesion means joining a text together with reference words
(e.g. he, theirs, the former) and conjunctions (e.g. but, then) so
that the whole text is clear and readable. This unit practises the
use of reference words, while conjunctions are examined in
Unit 3.5.

1 Reference words

These are used to avoid repetition:

> **Leonardo da Vinci** was a fifteenth-century Italian genius who
> produced only a handful of **finished works**. However, **they**
> include the **Mona Lisa** and the Last Supper, **the former** perhaps
> the most famous painting in the world. Although **he** is
> remembered mainly as an artist, **he** also was an innovative
> engineer, scientist and anatomist.

Here the reference words function as follows:

Leonardo da Vinci	finished works	Mona Lisa
he	they	the former

Examples of reference words and phrases

Pronouns	he/ she/ it/ they
Possessive pronouns	his/ her/ hers/ its/ their/ theirs
Objective pronouns	her/ him/ them
Demonstrative pronouns	this/ that/ these/ those
Other phrases	the former/ the latter/ the first/ the second/ such a

2 Practice A

■ Read the following paragraph and complete the table.

2.1 La Ferrera (1997) has researched the life cycle **of new businesses**. **She** found that **they** have an **average life of only 4.7 years**. **This** is due to two main reasons; one **economic** and one **social**. **The former** appears to be a lack of capital, **the latte**r a failure to carry out sufficient market research. La Ferrera considers that together **these** account for approximately 70 per cent of business failures.

Reference	Reference word/ phrase
La Ferrera	*She*
new businesses	
average life of only 4.7 years	
one economic	
one social	
the former. . ., the latter. . .	

3 Preventing confusion

To avoid confusing the reader it is important to use reference words only when the reference is clear. For example:

> Pablo Picasso moved to Paris in 1904 and worked with George Braque from 1908 to 1909. **He** became interested in the analysis of form, which led to cubism.

In this case it is not clear which person (Picasso or Braque) 'he' refers to. So to avoid this write:

> Pablo Picasso moved to Paris in 1904 and worked with George Braque from 1908 to 1909. **Picasso** became interested in the analysis of form, which led to cubism.

4 Practice B

■ In the following paragraph, insert suitable reference words from the box below in the gaps (more words than gaps).

> **he / he / his / his / his / it / them / they / this**

4.1   FAMOUS FOR ?

When Andy Warhol died at the age of 58 in 1987 few people guessed that (a)_____ would soon become one of the most valuable artists in the world. In 2007 total sales of (b)_____ work at auction reached 428 million dollars. When, a year later, (c)_____ painting 'Eight Elvises' sold for over $100 million, (d)_____ was one of the highest prices ever paid for a work of art. In (e)_____ working life (f)_____ made about 10,000 artworks, and dealers believe that (g)_____ will continue to be popular with collectors in future. (h)_____ is because of Warhol's huge reputation as a super-cool trendsetter and innovator.

5 Practice C

■ Read the paragraph below and replace the words in bold with reference words.

5.1　VELCRO

Velcro is a fabric fastener used with clothes and shoes. **Velcro** was invented by a Swiss engineer called George de Mestral. **Mestral's** idea was derived from studying the tiny hooks found on some plant seeds. **The tiny hooks** cling to animals and help disperse the seeds. Mestral spent eight years perfecting **Mestral's** invention, which **Mestral** called 'Velcro' from the French words 'velour' and 'crochet'. **The invention** was patented in 1955 and today over 60 million metres of Velcro are sold annually.

6 Practice D

■ Use the following information to write a paragraph about nylon, paying careful attention to the use of reference words.

Nylon

Inventor:	Wallace Carothers
Company:	DuPont Corporation (USA)
Carothers' position:	Director of research centre
Carothers' background:	Chemistry student, specialising in polymers (molecules composed of long chains of atoms)
Properties:	Strong but fine synthetic fibre
Patented:	1935
Mass produced:	1939
Applications:	Stockings, toothbrushes, parachutes, fishing lines, surgical thread

CHAPTER 2.4 Comparisons

> It is often necessary to make comparisons in academic writing. The comparison might be the subject of the essay, or might provide evidence for the argument. In all cases it is important to explain clearly what is being compared and to make the comparison as accurate as possible. This unit deals with different forms of comparison and practises their use.

1 Comparison structures

(a) Some studies are based on a comparison:

> The purpose of this study is to compare Chinese and American consumers on their propensity to use self-service technology in a retail setting . . .

In other cases a comparison provides useful context:

> The first attempt to decode the human genome took 10 years; now it can be done in less than a week.

(b) The two basic comparative forms are:

> (i) France is **larger** than Switzerland.
> The students were **happier** after the exam.

(*-er* is added to one-syllable adjectives and two-syllable adjectives ending in *-y*, which changes into an *i*)

(ii) Learning Chinese is **more difficult** than learning English.

(*more . . .* is used with other adjectives of two or more syllables)

(c) These comparisons can be modified by the use of adverbs such as *slightly, considerably, significantly* and *substantially*:

France is **substantially larger** than Switzerland.

Switzerland is **slightly smaller** than Holland.

Winters in Poland are **significantly colder** than in Portugal.

(d) Similarity can be noted by the use of *as . . . as* or *the same as*:

The population of France is **the same as** the population of Britain.

Summers in Tokyo are **as wet as** in Singapore.

This form can be used for quantitative comparison:

Britain is half **as large as** France. (also twice as large as, ten times as fast as)

2 Practice A

■ **Study the table on the next page, which shows the price of quality residential property in various cities. Complete the following comparisons, and write two more.**

(a) Residential property in London is twice as expensive _____ in Rome.

(b) Property in Moscow is _____ cheaper than in New York.

(c) Tokyo property is nearly as expensive as property in _____ .

(d) Singapore has significantly cheaper property _____ New York.

€ per sq. m.	City
28,000	London
16,500	New York
16,200	Moscow
16,000	Paris
15,850	Tokyo
13,500	Rome
11,850	Singapore
11,000	Sydney

(e) London is the _____ expensive of the eight cities, while Sydney is the cheapest.

(f) _____

_____

(g) _____

_____

3 Forms of comparison

Compare these three possible forms:

Parisian property is more expensive than Roman (property).
Property in Paris is more expensive than in Rome.
The price of property in Paris is higher than in Rome.

Note that high/ low are used for comparing abstract ideas (e.g. rates)

The birth rate was **higher** 20 years ago.

more/ less must be used with *than + comparison*:

This module is **more difficult** than the last one.
Divorce is **less common** in Turkey than in Germany.

4 Using superlatives (e.g. the largest/ smallest)

When using superlatives take care to define the group, e.g. 'the cheapest car' has no meaning:

> the cheapest car **in the Ford range**/ the fastest car **in the USA**

the most/ the least are followed by an adjective:

> the **most interesting** example is Ireland . . .

the most/ the fewest are used in relation to numbers:

> **the fewest** students studied biogenetics (i.e. the lowest number)

5 Practice B

■ Study the table, which shows the income of the top ten clubs in world football. Then read the comparisons. Each sentence contains one error. Find and correct it.

Club	Revenue € m. 2007–8
Real Madrid	366
Manchester United	310
FC Barcelona	304
Bayern Munich	295
Chelsea	270
Arsenal	265
Liverpool	210
AC Milan	205
AS Roma	180
Internazionale	175

(a) Real Madrid was the richest club.

(b) Real Madrid's income was twice much as AS Roma's.

(c) FC Barcelona earned significantly less than Manchester United.

(d) Internazionale had less revenue AC Milan.

(e) Liverpool's income was slightly lower than AC Milan's.

6 Practice C

■ **Study the table below and complete the gaps in the paragraph (one word per gap).**

Marriage and divorce rates (per 1,000 population).

Country	Marriage rate	Divorce rate
Egypt	10.6	1.5
United States	8.4	4.7
Iran	8.4	0.8
Turkey	8.3	0.6
Japan	6.2	1.9
Russia	5.2	2.9
Spain	5.2	0.8
United Kingdom	5.2	3.1
South Africa	4.0	0.9
Libya	3.9	0.3

The table (a) _____ marriage and divorce rates in a

variety of countries. The marriage (b) _____ ranges

from 10.6 per thousand in Egypt to 3.9 in Libya, while the rate of divorce (c) _____ even more, from 4.7 in the USA to

only 0.3 in Libya. The marriage rate in America is the (d)

_____ as in Iran, which has a (e) _____

higher rate (f) _____ Turkey's. In countries such as

Iran, Turkey and Libya only 10 per cent of marriages appear

to end in divorce, but in Russia and the USA the number

is (g) _____ half. It seems possible that the

(h) _____ marriage rate in the USA may be partly

due to second marriages.

7 Practice D

■ The table below compares the number of Nobel prize winners (Literature, Medicine and Physics) for eight countries between 1901 and 2002. Write comparative sentences based on this data.

Country	Literature	Medicine	Physics
USA	12	48	45
France	14	6	8
UK	9	21	19
Germany	7	14	17
Sweden	6	7	4
Italy	5	3	3
Russia	3	–	6
Switzerland	–	6	4

(a) *France had the highest number of prize winners*

   for Literature.

(b) _____

   _____

(c) _____

   _____

(d) _____

   _____

(e) _____

   _____

(f) _____

   _____

(g) _____

   _____

Definitions

Definitions are usually found in introductions (see Unit 1.11). They are not needed in every case, but if the title includes an unfamiliar phrase, or if the writer wants to use a term in a special way, it is important to make clear to the reader exactly what is meant in this context. This unit presents ways of writing both simple and complex definitions.

---

1 Simple definitions

Basic definitions are formed by giving a category and the application:

Word	Category	Application
An agenda	is a set of issues	to be discussed in a meeting
A master's degree	is an academic award	for post-graduate students, given on completion of a dissertation

■ **Complete the following definitions by inserting a suitable category word or phrase from the box (There are more words than gaps).**

> material   theory   behaviour   organisation   organs
>
> instrument   process   period   grains   profession

(a) A barometer is a scientific _____ designed to measure atmospheric pressure.

(b) Kidneys are _____ that separate waste fluid from the blood.

(c) A multi-national company is a business _____ that operates in many countries.

(d) Reinforced concrete is a building _____ consisting of cement, sand and steel rods.

(e) Bullying is a pattern of anti-social _____ found in many schools.

(f) Recycling is a _____ in which materials are used again.

(g) A recession is a _____ of reduced economic activity.

(h) Cereals are _____ widely grown for food production.

■ **Write definitions for the following:**

(i) A lecture is _____

_____

(j) Tuberculosis (TB) is _____

_____

(k) The Red Cross is _____

_____

(l) An idiom is _____

_____

2 Complex definitions

■ **Study the following examples and underline the term being defined.**

(a) The definition for a failed project ranges from abandoned projects to projects that do not meet their full potential or simply have schedule overrun problems.

(b) Development is a socio-economic-technological process having the main objective of raising the standards of living of the people.

(c) Bowlby (1982) suggested that attachment is an organised system whose goal is to make individuals feel safe and secure.

(d) . . . the non-linear effect called 'self-brightening' in which large-amplitude waves decay more slowly than small-amplitude ones . . .

(e) Globalisation, in an economic sense, describes the opening up of national economies to global markets and global capital, the freer movement and diffusion of goods, services, finance, people, knowledge and technology around the world.

These examples illustrate the variety of methods used in giving definitions.

■ **Which of the above**

(i)   quotes a definition from another writer?

(ii) gives a variety of relevant situations?

(iii) explains a process?

(iv) uses category words?

3 Practice

When writing introductions it is often useful to define a term in the title, even if it is fairly common, in order to demonstrate your understanding of its meaning.

Example:
Title: 'Higher education should be free and open to all – Discuss.'

Higher education usually means university-level study for first or higher degrees, normally at the age of 18 or above.

■ **Study the following titles, underline the terms that are worth defining, and write definitions for three of them.**

(a) Capital punishment has no place in the modern legal system – Discuss.

(b) How can the management of an entrepreneurial business retain its entrepreneurial culture as it matures?

(c) E-books are likely to replace printed books in the next twenty years. Do you agree?

(d) As urban areas continue to expand worldwide, will agriculture be able to feed the growing population of cities?

(e) Given the medical dangers of obesity, what is the best way of reducing its incidence?

1
2
3

Examples

Examples are used in academic writing for support and illustration. Suitable examples can strengthen the argument, and they can also help the reader to understand a point. This unit demonstrates the different ways in which examples can be introduced, and practises their use.

1 Using examples

Generalisations are commonly used to introduce a topic:

> Many plants and animals are threatened by global warming.

But if the reader is given an example for illustration the idea becomes more concrete:

> Many plants and animals are threatened by global warming. **Polar bears, for example, are suffering from the lack of Arctic ice.**

The example may also support the point the writer is making:

> A participatory public has been a defining feature of American politics and historically a strength of the political system.

Alexis de Tocqueville's classic treatise on 'Democracy in America' (1966) stressed the participatory tendencies of Americans in contrast to European publics.

▶ See Unit 2.7 Generalisations

2 Phrases to introduce examples

(a) **for instance, for example** (with commas)

Some car manufacturers, for instance Hyundai, now offer five-year guarantees.

(b) **such as, e.g.**

Many successful businessmen such as Bill Gates have no formal qualifications.

(c) **particularly, especially** (to give a focus)

Certain Masters courses, especially American ones, take two years.

(d) **a case in point** (for single examples)

A few diseases have been successfully eradicated. A case in point is smallpox.

■ Add a suitable example to each sentence and introduce it with one of the phrases above.

Examples:
A number of sports have become very profitable due to the sale of television rights.
A number of sports, **for instance motor racing**, have become very profitable due to the sale of television rights.

(a) Some twentieth-century inventions affected the lives of most people.

(b) Lately many countries have introduced fees for university courses.

(c) Various companies have built their reputation on the strength of one product.

(d) In recent years more women have become political leaders.

(e) Certain countries are frequently affected by earthquakes.

(f) Many musical instruments use strings to make music.

(g) A group of root crops constitute an important part of our diets.

(h) Politicians have discussed a range of possible alternative punishments to prison.

3 Practice A

■ **Study the following text and add examples from the box where suitable, using one of the introductory phrases in (2) above.**

free delivery or discounted prices
bookshops
clothing and footwear
books and music
many supermarkets offer delivery services for online customers

3.1 Widespread use of the internet has led to a major change in shopping habits. It is no longer necessary to visit shops to make routine purchases. With more specialised items internet retailers can offer a wider range of products than bricks-and-mortar shops. They can also provide extra incentives to customers, in addition to the convenience of not having to visit a real shop. As a result certain types of store are disappearing from the high street. Other products however, appear to require personal inspection and approval, and in addition many people enjoy the activity of shopping, so it seems unlikely that the internet will completely replace the shopping centre.

4 Practice B

■ **Read the text below and then insert suitable examples where needed.**

4.1 Students who go to study abroad often experience a type of culture shock when they arrive in the new country. Customs that they took for granted in their own society may not be followed in the host country. Even everyday patterns of life may be different. When these are added to the inevitable differences that occur in every country students may at first feel confused. They may experience rapid changes of mood, or even want to return home. However, most soon make new friends and, in a relatively short period, are able to adjust to their new environment. They may even find that they prefer some aspects of their new surroundings, and forget that they are not at home for a while!

5 Restatement

Another small group of phrases is used when there is only one 'example'. (Brackets may also be used for this purpose.) This is a kind of restatement to clarify the meaning:

> The world's leading gold producer **namely** South Africa has been faced with a number of technical difficulties.

in other words	namely	that is (to say)	i.e.	viz (very formal)

■ **Add a suitable phrase from the box below to the following sentences, to make them clearer.**

(a) The company's overheads doubled last year.

(b) The Roman empire was a period of autocratic rule.

(c) The Indian capital has a thriving commercial centre.

(d) Survival rates from the most common type of cancer are improving.

(e) Participation rates in most democracies are in decline.

that is to say fewer people are voting	(27 BC – 476 AD)
in other words the fixed costs	i.e. breast cancer
namely New Delhi	

Generalisations

> Generalisations are often used to introduce a topic. They can be powerful statements because they are simple and easy to understand. But they must be used with care, to avoid being inaccurate or too simplistic. This unit explains how to generalise clearly and effectively.

1 Using generalisations

(a) Generalisations are used to give a simple picture of a topic. Compare:

> The majority of smokers in Britain are women.

and

> Of all smokers in the UK, 56.2 per cent are women and 43.8 per cent are men.

Although the second sentence is more accurate, the first is easier to understand and remember. The writer must decide when accuracy is necessary, and when a generalisation will be acceptable.

(b) You must avoid using generalisations that cannot be supported by evidence or research, e.g. *Students tend to be lazy.*

■ **Decide which of the following are valid generalisations:**

(a) Cats are more intelligent than dogs.

(b) Earthquakes are difficult to predict.

(c) There is a link between poverty and disease.

(d) Women work harder than men.

(e) Air travel is faster than train travel.

2 Structure

Generalisations can be made in two ways:

(a) Most commonly using the plural:

Computers have transformed the way we live.

(b) Using the singular + definite article (more formal):

The computer has transformed the way we live.

Avoid absolute phrases in generalisations such as:

Young children learn second languages easily.

Such statements are dangerous because there may well be exceptions. Instead, it is better to use cautious phrases such as:

Young children tend to learn second languages easily.

▶ **See Unit 3.4 Caution**

■ **Read the following text and underline the generalisations.**

> **2.1** What we look for in choosing a mate seems to vary from place to place. A recent study (Jones and DeBruine, 2010) explores the idea that female preferences in a mate might vary according to the society in which she lives. In their research nearly 5,000 women in 30 countries were shown the same pictures of male faces and asked to state which they found more attractive. In countries where disease is common women chose men with more masculine features, while in countries such as America with more advanced health care and lower levels of disease, more effeminate-looking men were preferred. The researchers conclude that in healthier societies women are more interested in men who may form long-term relationships and help with child-rearing, while in places where child mortality rates are high they choose strongly-featured men who seem more likely to produce healthy children.

3 Practice A

■ **Write generalisations on the following topics.**

(a) fresh fruit/ health

   Eating fresh fruit is important for health.

(b) regular rainfall/ good crop yields

_____

(c) honest judges/ respect for the law

_____

(d) adequate sleep/ academic success

_____

(e) industrial growth/ pollution

_____

(f) cold weather/ demand for gas

_____

(g) job satisfaction/ interesting work

_____

4 Practice B

■ **Study the table and write five generalisations using the information.**

Results of a college survey on where students prefer to study.

	Undergraduates (%)		Graduates (%)	
	Male	Female	Male	Female
Library	20	17	47	32
Own room in silence	21	27	26	38
Own room with music	25	13	12	14
Own room in bed	15	24	6	10
Outdoors	6	9	4	2
Other	13	10	5	4

(a) _____

_____

(b) _____

_____

(c) _____

_____

(d) _____

_____

(e) _____

_____

5 Building on generalisations

Most essays move from the general to the specific, as a generalisation has to be supported and developed. For example, an essay with the title 'The impact of globalisation on the Chinese economy' might develop in this way:

Generalisation	Support	Development > Specific
Since the mid-twentieth century there has been a remarkable increase in international trade.	The reasons for this are a combination of international agreements such as GATT, better transport and improved communications.	China has played a significant part in this process, with its international trade growing by 16 times in just 20 years, while its GDP increased by nearly 10 per cent per year.

■ **Choose a title from the list below, or select one from your own subject, write a generalisation and develop it in the same way.**

(a) Does tourism always have a negative effect on the host country?

(b) Should governments use taxation to promote public health?

(c) Is it more important to protect forests or to grow food?

(d) Is it better for the state to spend money on primary or university education?

Generalisation	Support	Development > Specific

CHAPTER 2.8 Numbers

Most students are required to write about statistical data clearly and accurately. This unit explains and practises the basic language of numbers and percentages, while presenting data in charts and tables is dealt with in Unit 2.11 Visual information.

1 The language of numbers

In introductions numbers are often used to give an accurate account of a situation:

> Approximately 1800 children between the ages of five and 12 years were randomly selected . . .

> The earth's atmosphere appears to be gaining 3.3 billion metric tons of carbon annually . . .

> . . . but five winters in the twentieth century were more than 2.4°C colder than average

Figures and **numbers** are both used to talk about statistical data in a general sense:

> The **figures/ numbers** in the report need to be read critically.

But number is used more widely:

> 13 is an unlucky **number**.
>
> She forgot her phone **number**.

Digits are individual numbers.

> 4,539 – a four **digit** number.

Both **fractions** (1/2) and **decimals** (0.975) may be used.

There is no final 's' on hundred/ thousand/ million used with whole numbers:

> Six **million** people live there.
>
> *but:* **Thousands of** people were forced to move from the area.

When writing about **currencies** write *$440 m.* (440 million dollars).

Rates are normally expressed as percentages (e.g. *the literacy rate rose to 75%*) but may also be per thousand (e.g. *the Austrian birth rate is 8.7*).

It is normal to write whole numbers as words from one to ten and as digits above ten:

> **Five** people normally work in the café, but at peak times this can rise to **14**.

2 Percentages

These are commonly used for expressing degrees of change:

> Since 2008 the number of prisoners has risen by 22 per cent.

■ Complete the following sentences using the data in the table opposite.

(a) Between 2007 and 2008, the number of overseas students increased by _____ per cent.

(b) The number increased by _____ per cent the following year.

(c) Between 2007 and 2010 there was a _____ per cent increase.

Overseas students in the university 2007–2010

2007	2008	2009	2010
200	300	600	1000

3 Simplification

Although the accurate use of numbers is vital, too many statistics can make texts difficult to read. If the actual number is not important, words such as *various*, *dozens* or *scores* may be used instead:

> The snowstorm closed 47 schools.

> The snowstorm closed dozens of schools.

few	less than expected
a few	approximately 3–6 depending on context
several	approximately 3–4
various	approximately 4–6
dozens of	approximately 30–60
scores of	approximately 60–100

■ **Rewrite the following sentences using one of the words or phrases in the table above.**

(a) Only three people attended the meeting.

Few people attended the meeting.

(b) 77 students applied for the scholarship.

_____

(c) He re-wrote the essay three times.

_____

(d) Last year 38 books were published on biogenetics.

_____

(e) Five names were suggested but rejected for the new chocolate
bar.

_____

(f) The students thought of four good topics for their project.

_____

4 Further numerical phrases

The expressions listed below can also be used to present and simplify
statistical information. For example:

The course fees rose from $1,200 to $2,500 in two years.

could be written:

The course fees doubled in two years.

If appropriate, *roughly/ approximately* can be added:

The course fees roughly doubled in two years.

one in three	**one in three** engineering students is from China
twice/ three times as many	**twice as many** women as men study business law
a five/ tenfold increase	there was **a fivefold increase** in the price of oil
to double/ halve	the rate of infection **halved** after 2001
the highest/ lowest	**the lowest** rate of home ownership was in Germany
a quarter/ fifth	**a fifth** of all employees leave every year
the majority/ minority	**the majority** of births are in hospital
on average, the average	**on average**, each judge hears two cases per day
a small/ large proportion	the website generates **a large proportion** of their sales

NB. 5–20 per cent = a tiny/ small minority

21–39 per cent = a minority

40–49 per cent = a substantial/ significant minority

51–55 per cent = a small majority

56–79 per cent = a majority

80 per cent + = a large majority

■ **Re-write each sentence in a simpler way, using a suitable expression from the list above.**

(a) In 1975 a litre of petrol cost 12p, while the price is now £1.20.

_____

(b) Out of 18 students in the group 12 were women.

_____

(c) The new high-speed train reduced the journey time to Madrid from seven hours to three hours 20 minutes.

_____

(d) The number of students applying for the Psychology course has risen from 350 last year to 525 this year.

_____

(e) Visitor numbers to the theme park show a steady increase. In 2007 there were 40,000 admissions, in 2008 82,000 and 171,000 in 2009.

_____

(f) More than 80 per cent of British students complete their first degree course; in Italy the figure is just 35 per cent.

_____

(g) Tap water costs 0.07p per litre while bottled water costs, on average, 50p per litre.

_____

(h) The rate of unemployment ranges from 18 per cent in Spain to 3 per cent in Norway.

_____

(i) Seven out of every 100 computers produced had some kind of
     fault.

     _____

(j) 57 per cent of the members supported the suggestion, but
     83 per cent of these had some doubts.

     _____

5 Practice

■ **The following data was collected about a group of 15 international
students. Write sentences about the group using the data.**

Mother tongue		Future course		Age		Favourite sport	
Arabic	2	Architecture	1	21	1	climbing	2
Chinese	8	Economics	3	22	3	cycling	1
French	1	Education	2	23	9	dancing	3
Japanese	1	Maths	6	24	–	football	3
Korean	2	Physics	2	25	–	swimming	5
Spanish	1	Psychology	1	26	1	tennis	1

(a) *A small majority have Chinese as their mother tongue.*

(b) _____

(c) _____

(d) _____

(e) _____

(f) _____

Problems and solutions

Writing tasks frequently ask students to examine a problem and evaluate a range of solutions. This unit explains ways in which this kind of text can be organised. Note that some of the language is similar to that practised in Unit 2.1 Argument and discussion.

1 Structure

■ Study the organisation of the following paragraph:

1.1 HOW CAN ROAD CONGESTION BE REDUCED?

Currently, roads are often congested, which is expensive in terms of delays to the movement of people and freight. It is commonly suggested that building more roads, or widening existing ones, would ease the traffic jams. But not only is the cost of such work high, but the construction process adds to the congestion, while the resulting extra road space may encourage extra traffic. Therefore constructing more roads is unlikely to solve the problem, and other remedies, such as road pricing or greater use of public transport, should be examined.

(a) Problem	Currently, roads are often congested, which is . . .
(b) Solution A	It is commonly suggested that building more roads, or widening . . .
(c) Arguments against solution A	But not only is the cost of such work high, but . . .
(d) Solutions B and C	. . . other remedies, such as road pricing or greater use . . .

2 Alternative structure

The same ideas could be re-ordered to arrive at a different conclusion:

2.1   HOW CAN ROAD CONGESTION BE REDUCED?

Currently, roads are often congested, which is expensive in terms of delays to the movement of people and freight. It is commonly suggested that building more roads, or widening existing ones, would ease the traffic jams. This remedy is criticised for being expensive and liable to lead to more road use, which may be partly true, yet the alternatives are equally problematic. Road pricing has many practical difficulties, while people are reluctant to use public transport. There is little alternative to a road building programme except increasing road chaos.

Problem	Currently, roads are often congested, which is . . .
Solution A	It is commonly suggested that building more roads, or widening . . .
Arguments against solution A	This remedy is criticised for being expensive . . .
Solutions B and C and arguments against	Road pricing has many practical difficulties, while people are . . .
Conclusion in favour of solution A	There is little alternative to a road building programme . . .

3 Practice A

■ Analyse the following paragraph in a similar way:

> ### 3.1 MANAGING TOURISM GROWTH
>
> Many developing countries have found that the development of a tourism industry can bring social and environmental drawbacks. Growing visitor numbers can cause pollution and put pressure on scarce resources such as water. One possible solution is to target wealthier holidaymakers, in order to get the maximum profit from minimum numbers. However, there is a limited number of such visitors, and this market requires considerable investment in infrastructure and training. Another remedy is to rigorously control the environmental standards of any development, in order to minimise the impact of the construction. This requires effective government agencies, but is likely to ensure the best outcome for both tourists and locals.

Problem	
Solution A	
Argument against solution A	
Solution B	
Conclusion in favour of B	

4 Vocabulary

The following words can be used as synonyms for *problem* and *solution*.

three main **difficulties** have arisen . . .	the best **remedy** for this may be . . .
the main **challenge** faced by nurses . . .	two **answers** have been put forward . . .
one of the **concerns** during the recession . . .	another **suggestion** is . . .
the new process created two **questions** . . .	Matheson's **proposal** was finally accepted.
the team faced six **issues** . . .	this was finally **rectified** by . . .
our principal **worry/ dilemma** was . . .	

5 Practice B

◼ Use the following points to build an argument in one paragraph, using the box below.

Topic:	University expansion
Problem:	Demand for university places is growing, leading to overcrowding in lectures and seminars
Solution A:	Increase fees to reduce demand
Argument against A:	Unfair to poorer students
Solution B:	Government pays to expand universities
Argument against B:	Unfair to average taxpayer who would be subsidising the education of a minority who will earn high salaries
Conclusion:	Government should subsidise poorer students

University expansion

Currently there is increasing demand ...

---

6 Practice C

■ Think of a similar problem in your subject area. Complete the table and
   write a paragraph that leads to a conclusion.

Topic	
Problem	
Solution A	
Argument against A	
Solution B	
Argument for/against B	
(Solution C)	
Conclusion	

Style

There is no one correct style of academic writing, and students should aim to develop their own 'voice'. In general, it should attempt to be accurate, impersonal and objective. For example, personal pronouns like 'I' and idioms (i.e. informal language) are used less often than in other writing. This unit gives some guidelines for an appropriate style, but see also Units 3.2 Academic vocabulary, 3.4 Caution and 3.13 Verbs – passives.

1 Components of academic style

■ **Study this paragraph and underline any examples of poor style.**

1.1 How to make people work harder is a topic that lots of people have written about in the last few years. There are lots of different theories etc and I think some of them are ok. When we think about this we should remember the old Chinese proverb, that you can lead a horse to water but you can't make it drink. So how do we increase production? It's quite a complex subject but I'll just talk about a couple of ideas.

Some of the problems with the style of this paragraph can be analysed as follows:

How to make people work harder . . .	Imprecise vocabulary – use 'motivation'
. . . lots of people . . .	Vague – give names
. . . the last few years.	Vague – give dates
lots of different . . .	Avoid 'lots of'
. . . etc . . .	Avoid using 'etc' and 'and so on'
. . . I think . . .	Too personal
. . . are ok.	Too informal
When we think about this . . .	Too personal
. . . the old Chinese proverb . . .	Do not quote proverbs or similar expressions
So how do we increase production?	Avoid rhetorical questions
It's quite a . . .	Avoid contractions
. . . I'll just talk about a couple . . .	Too personal and informal

The paragraph could be re-written:

1.2   Motivation has been the subject of numerous studies during recent decades, but this essay will focus on Maslow's hierarchy of needs theory (1943) and Herzberg's two-factor theory (1966). Their contemporary relevance to the need to motivate employees effectively will be examined critically, given that this can be considered crucial to a firm's survival in the current economic climate.

2 Guidelines

There are no rules for academic style that apply to all situations. The following are guidelines that should help you develop a style of your own.

(a) Do not use idiomatic or colloquial vocabulary: *kids, boss*. Instead use standard English: *children, manager*.

(b) Use vocabulary accurately. There is a difference between *rule* and *law*, or *weather* and *climate*, which you are expected to know if you study these subjects.

(c) Be as precise as possible when dealing with facts or figures. Avoid phrases such as *about a hundred* or *hundreds of years ago*. If it is necessary to estimate numbers use *approximately* rather than *about*.

(d) Conclusions should use tentative language. Avoid absolute statements such as *unemployment causes crime*. Instead use cautious phrases: *unemployment may cause crime* or *tends to cause crime*.

▶ **See Unit 3.4 Caution**

(e) Avoid adverbs that show your personal attitude: *luckily, remarkably, surprisingly*.

(f) Do not contract verb forms: *don't, can't*. Use the full form: *Do not, cannot*.

(g) Although academic English tends to use the passive more than standard English, it should not be over-used. Both are needed. Compare:

Galileo discovered the moons of Jupiter.

The moons of Jupiter were discovered by Galileo.

In the first case, the focus is on Galileo, in the second (passive) on the moons.

▶ **See Unit 3.13 Verbs – passives**

(h) Avoid the following:

- *like* for introducing examples. Use *such as* or *for instance*.
- *thing* and combinations *nothing* or *something*. Use *factor, issue* or *topic*.
- *lots of*. Use *a significant / considerable number*.
- *little / big*. Use *small / large*.

- 'get' phrases such as *get better / worse*. Use *improve* and *deteriorate*.

- *good / bad* are simplistic. Use *positive / negative*, e.g. *the changes had several positive aspects*.

(i) Do not use question forms such as *Why did war break out in 1914? Instead use statements: There were three reasons for the outbreak of war . . .*

(j) Avoid numbering sections of your text, except in reports and long essays. Use conjunctions and signposting expressions to introduce new sections (*Turning to the question of detecting cancer . . .*).

(k) When writing lists, avoid using *etc* or *and so on*. Insert *and* before the last item:

The main products were pharmaceuticals, electronic goods and confectionery.

(l) Avoid using two-word verbs such as *go on* or *bring up* if there is a suitable synonym. Use *continue* or *raise*.

▶ **See Unit 3.2 Academic vocabulary**

3 Practice

■ **In the following sentences, underline examples of bad style and re-write them in a more suitable way.**

(a) Another thing to think about is the chance of crime getting worse.

_____

(b) Regrettably these days lots of people don't have jobs.

_____

(c) Sometime soon they will find a vaccine for malaria.

_____

(d) A few years ago the price of property in Japan went down a lot.

_____

(e) You can't always trust the numbers in that report.

_____

(f) Sadly, the high inflation led to poverty, social unrest and so on.

_____

(g) He was over the moon when he won the prize.

_____

(h) I think we should pay students to study.

_____

(i) A few years ago they allowed women to vote.

_____

(j) What were the main causes of the Russian revolution?

_____

4 Avoiding repetition and redundancy

Repetition means repeating a word instead of using a synonym to provide
variety, which makes the text more interesting. So instead of:

> Most family businesses employ less than ten people. These
> **businesses** . . .

Use:

> Most family businesses employ less than ten people. These
> **firms** . . .

▶ **See Unit 3.11 Synonyms**

Redundancy, i.e. repeating an idea or including an irrelevant point, suggests
that the writer is not fully in control of the material. It gives the impression
that either he does not properly understand the language or is trying to
'pad' the essay by repeating the same point. Avoid phrases such as:

> Homelessness is a global problem in the whole world.

Good writing aims for economy and precision:

> Homelessness is a global problem.

■ In the following text, remove all repetition and redundancy, re-writing
where necessary.

4.1   **FAST FOOD**

Currently these days, fast food is growing in popularity. Fast food is a kind of
food that people can buy ready to eat or cook quickly. This essay examines the
advantages of fast food and the drawbacks of fast food. First above all, fast food
is very convenient. Most of the people who work in offices are very busy, so that
they do not have time to go to their homes for lunch. But the people who work in
offices can eat in restaurants such as McDonalds, which are franchised in
hundreds of countries. In addition, the second benefit of fast food is its
cheapness. As it is produced in large quantities, this high volume means that the
companies can keep costs down. As a result fast food is usually less expensive
than a meal in a conventional restaurant.

---

5 Varying sentence length

Short sentences are clear and easy to read:

> Car scrappage schemes have been introduced in many
> countries.

But too many short sentences are monotonous:

> Car scrappage schemes have been introduced in many
> countries. They offer a subsidy to buyers of new cars. The
> buyers must scrap an old vehicle. The schemes are designed
> to stimulate the economy. They also increase fuel efficiency.

Long sentences are more interesting but can be difficult to construct and
read:

> Car scrappage schemes, which offer a subsidy to buyers of
> new cars, who must scrap an old vehicle, have been
> introduced in many countries; the schemes are designed to
> stimulate the economy and also increase fuel efficiency.

Effective writing normally uses a mixture of long and short sentences, often using a short sentence to introduce the topic:

> Car scrappage schemes have been introduced in many countries. They offer a subsidy to buyers of new cars, who must scrap an old vehicle. The schemes are designed to stimulate the economy and also increase fuel efficiency.

■ **Re-write the following paragraph so that instead of six short sentences there are two long and two short sentences.**

5.1 Worldwide, enrolments in higher education are increasing. In developed countries over half of all young people enter college. Similar trends are seen in China and South America. This growth has put financial strain on state university systems. Many countries are asking students and parents to contribute. This leads to a debate about whether students or society benefit from tertiary education.

■ **The following sentence is too long. Divide it into shorter ones.**

5.2 China is one developing country (but not the only one) which has imposed fees on students since 1997, but the results have been surprising: enrolments, especially in the most expensive universities, have continued to rise steeply, growing 200 per cent overall between 1997 and 2001; it seems in this case that higher fees attract rather than discourage students, who see them as a sign of a good education, and compete more fiercely for places, leading to the result that a place at a good college can cost $5000 per year for fees and maintenance.

Until you feel confident in your writing, it is better to use shorter rather than longer sentences. This should make your meaning as clear as possible.

Visual information

In many assignments it is essential to support your arguments with statistics. Visual devices such as graphs and tables are a convenient way of displaying large quantities of information in a form that is easy to understand. This unit explains and practises the language connected with these devices.

1 The language of change

(past tenses in brackets)

Verb ↗	Adverb	Verb ↘	Adjective + noun
grow (grew)	slightly	drop (dropped)	a slight drop
rise (rose)	gradually	fall (fell)	a gradual fall
increase (increased)	steadily	decrease (decreased)	a sharp decrease
climb (climbed)	sharply	decline (declined)	a steady decline
also: a peak, to peak, a plateau, to level off, a trough			

Average temperatures **rose steadily** until 2006 and then **dropped slightly**.

There was a **sharp decrease** in sales during the summer and then a **gradual rise**.

■ Study the graph below and complete the description with phrases from the table opposite.

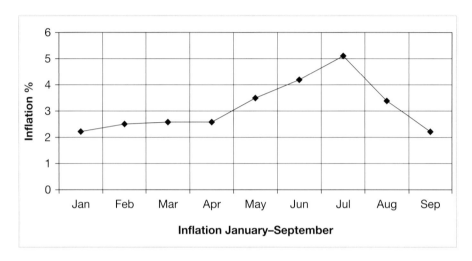

The graph shows that inflation (a) _____ slightly between January and February and then (b) _____ until April. It subsequently climbed (c) _____ to July, when it (d) _____ at just over 5 per cent. From July to September inflation (e) _____ steeply.

2 Types of visuals

■ On pp. 160–161 are examples of some of the main types of visuals used in academic texts. Complete the table to show the use (a–f) and the example (A–F) of each type.

Uses: (a) location

(b) comparison

(c) proportion

(d) function

(e) changes in time

(f) statistical display

TYPES	USES	EXAMPLE
1 diagram		
2 table		
3 map		
4 pie chart		
5 bar chart		
6 line graph		

(A) Cinema ticket sales

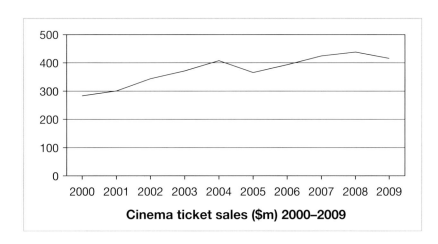

Cinema ticket sales ($m) 2000–2009

(B) Average life expectancy (in years)

Japan	81.6
France	79.0
United States	77.1
South Korea	75.5
Ghana	57.9
South Africa	47.7
Kenya	44.6
Zimbabwe	33.1

(C) Electricity output
    from coal

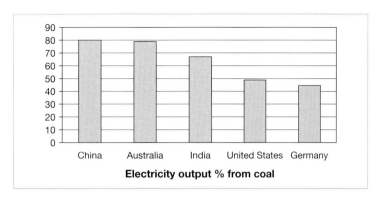

(D) Origins of international
    students

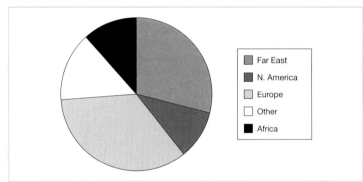

(E) Structure of the
    research unit

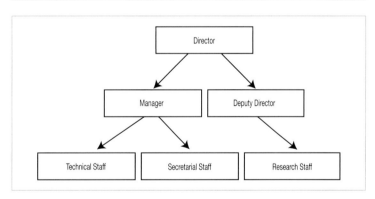

(F) Position of the main
    library

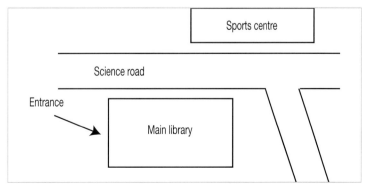

3 Describing visuals

Although visuals do largely speak for themselves, it is common to help the reader interpret them by briefly commenting on their main features.

The graph	shows	the changes in the price of oil since 1990
map	illustrates	the main sources of copper in Africa
diagram	displays	the organisation of both companies

■ **(a) Read the following descriptions of the chart below. Which is better, and why?**

(i)   The chart shows the quantity of tea consumed by the world's leading tea consuming nations. India and China together consume more than half the world's tea production, with India alone consuming about one third. Other significant tea consumers are Turkey, Russia and Britain. 'Others' includes the United States, Iran and Egypt.

(ii) The chart shows that 31 per cent of the world's tea is consumed by India, 23 per cent by China, and 8 per cent by Turkey. The fourth largest consumers are Russia, Japan and Britain, with 7 per cent each, while Pakistan consumes 5 per cent. Other countries account for the remaining 12 per cent.

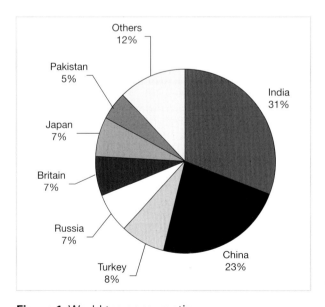

(Source: The Tea Council)

Figure 1 World tea consumption

■ (b) Complete the description of the chart below.

The bar chart shows population (a) _____ in a
variety of countries around the world. It (b) _____
the extreme contrast (c) _____ crowded nations
such as South Korea (475 people per sq. km.) and much
(d) _____ countries such as Canada (3 people
per sq. km.). Clearly, climate plays a major (e) _____
in determining population density, (f) _____ the
least crowded nations (g) _____ to have extreme
climates (e.g. cold in Russia or dry in Algeria).

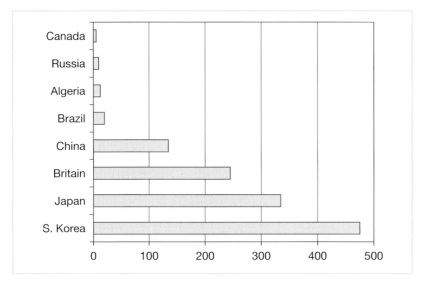

Figure 2 Population density (people per square kilometre)
(Source: OECD)

4 Labelling

- When referring to visual information in the text, the word 'figure' is used for almost everything (such as maps, charts and graphs) except tables (see examples above).

- Figures and tables should be numbered and given a title. Titles of tables are written above, while titles of figures are written below the data.

- As with other data, sources must be given for all visual information.

- If you are writing a lengthy work such as a dissertation you will need to provide lists of tables and figures, showing numbers, titles and page numbers after the contents page.

5 Practice A

■ Complete the following description of the table below (one word per gap).

Projected population changes in various European countries 2010–2050 (millions).

Country	Population 2010	Projected population 2050	Change
France	62	67	+ 5
Germany	82	71	– 11
Italy	60	57	– 3
Poland	38	32	– 6
Portugal	10.7	10	– 0.7
Russia	140	116	– 24
Spain	45	51	+ 6
UK	61	72	+ 10

(Source: UN)

The table (a) _____ the projected population

changes in (b) _____ European countries

(c) _____ 2010 and 2050. It can be seen that in a

(d) _____ the population is expected to fall, in some

cases (i.e. Germany and Russia) quite (e) _____.

However, the population of France, (f) _____ and

the UK is predicted to increase, in the case of the last two by

more (g) _____ 5 per cent.

6 Practice B

■ Write a paragraph commenting on the data in the table below.

Student survey of library facilities: percentage of students rating facilities as good.

Library facilities	Undergraduates	Postgraduates
Opening hours	72	63
Staff helpfulness	94	81
Ease of using electronic catalogue	65	87
Availability of working space	80	76
Café area	91	95
Availability of short loan stock	43	35
Quality of main book stock	69	54

(Source: Author)

Working in groups

Some university courses expect students to complete written assignments as part of a group of four to eight students. This unit explains the reasons for this, and suggests the best way to approach group work in order to achieve the maximum benefit from the process.

1 Why work in groups?

■ **Read the following text on p. 167. Working in pairs, and without looking back at the text, decide if the following are true or false.**

(a) All students react positively to the idea of group work.

(b) Each group member always receives the same mark.

(c) Students in groups can normally choose who they work with.

(d) There are two main reasons for setting group work.

(e) Most employers look for effective team members.

(f) Group work at university has no connection to team work in companies.

1.1   THE IMPORTANCE OF GROUP WORK

Students studying in English-medium institutions, especially those from other cultures, may be surprised to find they are expected to work in groups to complete some academic assignments. For those who have always worked on their own this may cause a kind of culture shock, especially as all the students in the group will normally be given the same mark for the group's work. In addition, students are normally told who they will work with, although the group may be able to choose its own topic with some kinds of project. However, there are important reasons for this emphasis on group work on many courses.

First of all, employers are generally looking for people who can work in a team. Most managers seek to employ people who are comfortable working in a mixed group with different skills and backgrounds. So ability to teamwork has become an essential qualification for many jobs, and this task provides students with an opportunity to strengthen their experience of working in groups.

Furthermore, working in groups allows individuals to achieve more than they could by working on their own. A group can tackle much larger projects, and this applies to most research projects at university, as well as business development in companies. Finally, by taking part in these activities students are able to provide evidence on their portfolio and CV that they have succeeded in this critical area.

2 Making group work successful

■ Below is a list of suggestions for making your group work successful. The correct order (1–7) has been mixed up. Working with a partner, put them into the most logical sequence, using the box below.

Analyse the task
Get everyone to discuss the assignment and agree on the best methods to complete it. At this stage it is important to have full agreement on the objectives.

Divide up the work fairly, according to the abilities of the members
Your group may include a computer expert or a design genius, so make sure that their talents are used for the benefit of the task. It is most important to make sure that everyone feels they have been given a fair share of the work.

Make everyone feel included
Nobody should feel an outsider, so make special efforts if there is only one male student, or one non-native speaker, for instance. Make a list of all members' phone numbers and email addresses and give everyone a copy.

Finish the assignment on time
This is the most important test of your group's performance. When you have finished and handed in your work, it may be helpful to have a final meeting to discuss what you have all learned from the task.

Get to know the other members
Normally you cannot choose who you work with, so it is crucial to introduce yourselves before starting work. Meet informally in a café or similar (but be careful not to choose a meeting place that may make some members uncomfortable, such as a bar).

Select a co-ordinator/ editor
Someone needs to take notes about what was agreed at meetings and send these to all members as a reminder. The same person could also act as editor, to make sure that all the individual sections conform to the same layout and format. However, you should each be responsible for proof-reading your own work.

Plan the job and the responsibilities
Break down the task week by week and allocate specific roles
to each member. Agree on times for regular meetings –
although you may be able to avoid some meetings by using
group emails. You may want to book a suitable room, for
example in the library, to hold your meetings.

1	
2	
3	
4	
5	*Divide up the work fairly, according to the abilities of the members*
6	
7	

3 Dealing with problems

■ Working in groups of three, discuss the best response to the following
situations. You may choose an alternative strategy to the ones
provided.

(a) In a group of six, you find that two students are not doing any
work. Not only do they not come to meetings, they have
not done the tasks they were given at the beginning. Should
you . . .

   (i)   Decide that it's simplest to do the work of the missing
students yourself?

  (ii) Find the students and explain that their behaviour is going
to damage the chances of all six members?

(iii) Tell your lecturer about the problem?

(b) You are the only non-native speaker in the group. Although you can understand normal speech, the other students speak so fast and idiomatically that you have difficulty taking part in the discussions. Should you . . .

(i) Tell your lecturer about the problem?

(ii) Keep quiet and ask another student in the group to explain decisions later?

(iii) Explain your problem to the group and ask them to speak more slowly?

(c) One member of the group is very dominant. He/ she attempts to control the group and is intolerant of the opinions of others. Should you . . .

(i) Explain to that person, in a group meeting, that their behaviour is having a negative effect on the group's task?

(ii) Tell your lecturer about the problem?

(iii) Let them do all the work, because that's what they seem to want?

4 Points to remember

- Working in groups is an ideal opportunity to make new friends – make the most of it.

- You may learn a lot by listening to other people's ideas.

- Negotiation is important in a group – nobody is right all the time.

- Respect the values and attitudes of others, especially people from different cultures – you may be surprised what you learn.

- Keep a record of your group work experience for inclusion in your portfolio of personal development (PPD) – to show to potential employers.

5 Practice

■ **Your teacher will put you in groups of 3–4. Together you have one week to research the history and development of the town or city where you are studying, using the internet, and write a 1,000 word report. Remember to follow the steps listed in (2) above.**

Your teacher will assess the report using the following criteria:

	Very good	Good	Satisfactory	Poor
Content: how well the different stages of development are explained and organised				
Accuracy and clarity of language and suitability of style				
Integration of individual contributions in overall report				

Accuracy in writing

CHAPTER 3.1 Abbreviations

> Abbreviations are an important and expanding feature of contemporary English, widely used for convenience and space-saving. Students need to be familiar with general and academic abbreviations.

1 Types of abbreviation

Abbreviations take the form of shortened words, acronyms or other abbreviations, as shown below.

(a) **Shortened words** are often used without the writer being aware of the original form. 'Bus' comes from 'omnibus', which is hardly used in modern English. However, 'refrigerator' is still better in written English than the informal 'fridge'. 'Public house' is now very formal ('pub' is acceptable), but 'television' or 'TV' should be used instead of the idiomatic 'telly'.

(b) **Acronyms** are made up of the initial letters of a name or phrase (e.g. AIDS = Acquired Immune Deficiency Syndrome). They are pronounced as words.

(c) **Other abbreviations** are read as sets of individual letters. They include names of countries, organisations and companies (USA/ BBC/ IBM), and also abbreviations that are only found in written English (e.g. PTO means 'please turn over'). Note that in many cases abbreviations are widely used without most users knowing what the individual letters stand for (e.g. DNA, DVD).

2 Some common abbreviations

AGM	annual general meeting
BA	Bachelor of Arts
BSc	Bachelor of Sciences
CV	curriculum vitae
DIY	do-it-yourself
EU	European Union
FE	further education (non-university study above 18)
GM	genetically modified
GNP	gross national product
HE	higher education (university study above 18)
HRM	human resource management
ICT	information and communications technology
IMF	International Monetary Fund
LLB	Bachelor of Laws
MA	Master of Arts
MSc	Master of Science
PG	Postgraduate
PGCE	Postgraduate Certificate of Education
PhD	Doctor of Philosophy
PLC	public limited company
PR	public relations
UCAS	Universities and Colleges Admissions Service
UG	undergraduate
UN	United Nations
URL	uniform resource locator (website address)
VC	Vice-Chancellor
WTO	World Trade Organisation

However, writers also employ more specialised abbreviations in texts, which are explained in brackets on first use:

Starting from the resource-based view (RBV) of the firm, it is argued that . . .

The Technology Readiness Index (TRI) was introduced by Parasuraman (2000).

3 Punctuation

There are many standard abbreviations that have a full stop after them to show that it is a shortened form (*lt.* = litre). Other examples are *govt.* (government), *co.* (company) and *Oct.* (October). With acronyms and other abbreviations there is no standard pattern for using full stops, so both BBC and B.B.C. are used. There is, however, a tendency to use full stops less. The important thing is to employ a consistent style in your work.

4 Duplicate abbreviations

Abbreviations can be confusing. PC, for example, may stand for 'personal computer' but also 'politically correct' or 'Police Constable'. It is useful to be aware of these potential confusions. A good dictionary should be used to understand more unusual abbreviations.

5 Abbreviations in writing

Certain abbreviations are found in all types of academic writing. They include:

anon.	anonymous (no author)
asap	as soon as possible
cf.	compare
ed.	editor/ edition
e.g.	for example
et al.	and others (used for giving names of multiple authors)
Fig.	figure (for labelling charts and graphs)
ibid.	in the same place (to refer to source mentioned immediately before)
i.e.	that is
K	thousand
NB.	take careful note
nd.	no date (i.e. an undated source)
op. cit.	in the source mentioned previously
p.a.	yearly (per annum)
pp.	pages
PS	postscript
re.	with reference to

6 Practice

■ **Explain the abbreviations in the following sentences.**

(a) The failure rate among ICT projects in HE reaches 40 per cent (Smith *et al.*, 2008).

(b) GM technology is leading to advances in many fields e.g. forestry.

(c) The world's most populous country (i.e. China) joined the WTO in 2001.

(d) NB. CVs must be submitted to HR by 30 June.

(e) See the OECD's recent report on the UAE.

(f) The EU hopes to achieve a standard rate of VAT.

(g) Her PhD examined the threat of TB in SE Asia.

(h) Fig. 4. Trade patterns on the www (2003–2008).

(i) The VC is meeting the PGCE students.

(j) Director of PR required – salary approx. $75K.

(k) Re. the AGM next month: the report is needed asap.

(l) Prof. Wren claimed that the quality of MSc and MA research was falling.

3.2 Academic vocabulary

To read and write academic texts effectively students need to be familiar with the rather formal vocabulary widely used in this area. This unit gives some examples, and provides practice in their use. See also Unit 3.6 Nouns and adjectives.

1 Adjectives, nouns and verbs

The table on the next page shows examples of some of the more common items.

■ **Use a dictionary to check that you understand them all.**

2 Practice A

■ **Choose the most suitable word ending in each case.**

(a) In the 1950s nuclear power was pred_____ to be cheap and clean.

(b) A signif_____ number of students have chosen to do that project.

(c) The rate of increase var_____ between 5 per cent and 8 per cent during the 1990s.

Adjective	Noun	Verb
achievable	achievement	achieve
acquired	acquisition	acquire
analytical	analysis	analyse
contributory	contribution/ contributor	contribute
creative	creation	create
definitive	definition	define
derived	derivation	derive
distributive	distribution/ distributor	distribute
emphatic	emphasis	emphasise
evaluative	evaluation	evaluate
hypothetical	hypothesis	hypothesise
indicative	indication/ indicator	indicate
interpretative	interpretation	interpret
invested	investment	invest
predictive	prediction/ predictor	predict
reliable	reliability	rely
responsive	response	respond
significant	significance	signify
synthetic	synthesis	synthesise
variable	variation/ variable	vary

(d) The first computer was creat_____ during the
    second world war.

(e) Researchers frequently need to ask hypoth_____
    questions.

(f) She invest_____ all her capital in the business.

(g) The company puts emph_____ on the
    reliab_____ of its products.

(h) The essays were evaluat_____ in terms of content
    and accuracy.

(i) Nylon was one of the first syn_____ fabrics in
    common use.

(j) Gandhi made a significant cont_____ to Indian
    history.

3 Practice B

■ Complete each sentence with a suitable word from the table on p. 180.

(a) The experiment's results were confusing; each researcher had her own _____.

(b) The word 'algebra' is _____ from Arabic.

(c) They received the Nobel Prize for their _____ in developing a new vaccine.

(d) Dr Wagner published the _____ work on South Asian snakes last year.

(e) Over 3,500 questionnaires were _____ in terms of social class.

(f) Three _____ need to be considered when forecasting an economic upturn.

4 Academic adjectives

The following adjectives are best understood and learnt as opposites:

absolute	relative
abstract	concrete
logical	illogical
metaphorical	literal
precise	vague or approximate or rough
rational	irrational
relevant	irrelevant
subjective	objective
theoretical	practical or empirical or pragmatic

Inflation is an **abstract** concept.

The **metaphorical** use of the word 'key' is probably more common than its **literal** one.

The study of engineering is very **relevant** to architecture.

Her study of women in education was criticised for being too **subjective**.

In Europe, **empirical** research began in the sixteenth century.

5 Practice C

■ **Complete each sentence with a suitable adjective from the table in (4).**

(a) The teacher complained that the quotes were
_____ to the title.

(b) His _____ approach led him to ignore
some inconvenient facts.

(c) _____ examples are needed to make
the argument clear.

(d) It is sufficient to give _____ figures
for national populations.

(e) Poverty is usually regarded as a _____
concept.

(f) They approached the task in a _____
way by first analysing the title.

(g) The students preferred examining case studies to
_____ discussion.

▶ **See Unit 3.6 Nouns and adjectives**

6 Formality in verbs

Academic writing tends to use rather formal verbs to express the writer's
meaning accurately:

> In the last decade the pace of change **accelerated**.

> Could Darwin have **envisaged** the controversy his work has
> caused?

In spoken English we are more likely to use 'speed up' and 'imagined'.

■ **Study the list below and find a synonym in each case.**

(Some of these verbs e.g. 'hold' are used in academic writing with a special
meaning.)

Verb	Example of use
to adapt	the health system has been **adapted** from France
to arise	a similar situation **arises** when we look at younger children
to conduct	the largest study was **conducted** in Finland
to characterise	developing countries are **characterised** by . . .
to clarify	the project was designed to **clarify** these contradictions
to concentrate on	that study **concentrated on** older children
to be concerned with	the programme is **concerned** primarily **with** . . .
to demonstrate	further research has **demonstrated** that few factors . . .
to determine	the water content was experimentally **determined**
to discriminate	a failure to **discriminate** between the two species
to establish	the northern boundary was **established** first
to exhibit	half of the patients **exhibited** signs of improvement
to focus on	her work **focused on** female managers
to generate	a question which has **generated** a range of responses
to hold	Newton's second Law, $F=ma$, **holds** everywhere
to identify	three main areas have been **identified**
to imply	his absence **implies** a lack of interest
to interact	understand how the two systems **interact**
to interpret	the result can be **interpreted** as a limited success
to manifest	as **manifested** in anti-social behaviour
to overcome	both difficulties were **overcome** in the first week
to propose	they **propose** that social class is the main factor
to prove	the use of solar power is **proving** successful
to recognise	he is now **recognised** as a leading expert
to relate to	the pattern was **related to** both social and physical factors
to supplement	the diet was **supplemented** with calcium and iodine
to undergo	the system **underwent** major changes in the 1980s
to yield	both surveys **yielded** mixed results

Students wishing to develop their academic vocabulary should study the Academic Word List (AWL). This is a list of 570 items commonly found in academic texts across various disciplines, created by Averil Coxhead.

See Sandra Haywood's website for information about the AWL, with further practice exercises: http://nottingham.ac.uk/~alzsh3/acvocab/

@   Academic vocabulary>

CHAPTER 3.3 **Articles**

Students often find the rules for using articles ('a', 'an' and 'the') confusing. This unit focuses on the definite article, 'the', and provides examples and practice.

1 Use of articles

Unless they are uncountable, all nouns need an article when used in the singular. The article can be either **a/an** or **the**. Compare:

(a) Research is an important activity in universities.

(b) **The** research begun by Dr Mathews was continued by Professor Brankovic.

(c) **An** interesting piece of research was conducted among 200 patients in the clinic.

In (a) research, which is usually uncountable, is being used in a general sense.

In (b) a specific piece of research is identified.

In (c) the research is being mentioned for the first time, and the word 'piece' is used to 'count' the research.

2 Using definite articles

■ i) Decide why the is used, or not used, in the following examples.

(a) The world's fastest animal is the cheetah.

(b) The USA was founded in the eighteenth century.

(c) The government increased taxation in the 1970s.

(d) The French Revolution was partly caused by bad harvests.

(e) The *New Scientist* is published every week.

(f) The south is characterised by poverty and emigration.

(g) Pablo Picasso, the Spanish artist, was born in Malaga.

(h) The River Seine runs through the middle of Paris.

(i) The United Nations was founded in 1945.

(j) The euro was introduced in 2002.

ii) In general, the is used with:

(a) superlatives *(fastest)*

(b) time periods *(eighteenth century/ 1970s)*

(c) unique things *(government, world)*

(d) specified things *(French Revolution)*

(e) regular publications *(New Scientist)*

(f) regions and rivers *(south/ River Seine)*

(g) very well-known people and things *(Spanish artist)*

(h) institutions and bodies *(United Nations)*

(i) positions *(middle)*

(j) currencies *(euro)*

It is **not** used with:

(k) things in general *(bad harvests)*

(l) names of countries, except for the UK, the USA and a few others

(m) abstract nouns e.g. poverty

(n) companies/ things named after people/ places e.g. Sainsbury's, Heathrow airport

Note the alternate forms:

> The deserts of Australia are expanding.
>
> Australian deserts/ Australia's deserts are expanding.

3 Practice A

◼ **In the following sentences, decide if the words and phrases underlined are specific or not, and whether 'the' should be added.**

Example:

> _____ inflation was the greatest problem
> for _____ Brazilian government.
>
> Inflation was the greatest problem for **the** Brazilian government.

(a) _____ engineering is the main industry
in _____ northern region.

(b) _____ insurance firms have made record profits
in _____ last decade.

(c) _____ global warming is partly caused by
_____ fossil fuels.

(d) _____ mayor has been arrested on _____
suspicion of corruption.

(e) _____ moons of Jupiter were discovered in
_____ eighteenth century.

(f) _____ tourism is _____ world's biggest
industry.

(g) _____ forests of Scandinavia produce most of
_____ Britain's paper.

(h) _____ Thai currency is _____ baht.

(i) _____ computer crime has grown by 200%
    in _____ last decade.

(j) _____ main causes of _____ industrial
    revolution are still debated.

(k) Already 3 per cent of _____ working population are
    employed in _____ call centres.

(l) _____ latest forecast predicts _____ warmer
    winters in _____ next five years.

(m) Research on _____ energy saving is being conducted
    in _____ Physics Faculty.

(n) _____ best definition is often _____ simplest.

4 Practice B

■ Complete the following text by inserting a/ an/ the (or nothing) in
  each gap. (Note that in some cases more than one answer is possible).

THE ORIGINS OF @

Giorio Stabile, (a) _____ professor of (b) _____
history at La Sapienza University in Rome, has demonstrated that
(c) _____ @ sign, now used in email addresses, was
actually invented 500 years ago. Professor Stabile has shown that
(d) _____ @, now (e) _____ symbol of
(f) _____ internet, was first used by (g) _____
Italian merchants during (h) _____ sixteenth century.

He claims that it originally represented (i) _____ unit of
volume, based on (j) _____ large jars used to carry liquids
in (k) _____ ancient Mediterranean world. He has found
(l) _____ first example of its use in (m) _____ letter
written in 1546 by (n) _____ merchant from Florence.
(o) _____ letter, which was sent to Rome, announces (p)
_____ arrival in Spain of (q) _____ ships carrying
gold from (r) _____ South America.

Caution

The need to avoid absolute statements was mentioned in
Unit 2.10 Style. This unit presents more examples of tentative
or cautious language, using modal verbs, adverbs and verbs,
and practises its use.

1 The use of caution

A cautious style is necessary in many areas of academic writing to avoid
making statements that can be contradicted:

> Demand for healthcare **usually** exceeds supply.
>
> **Most** students find writing exam essays difficult.
>
> Fertility rates **tend to** fall as societies get richer.

Areas where caution is particularly important include:

(a) outlining a hypothesis that needs to be tested (e.g. in an introduction)

(b) discussing the results of a study, which may not be conclusive

(c) commenting on the work of other writers

(d) making predictions (normally with **may** or **might**)

2 The language of caution

Caution is also needed to avoid making statements that are too simplistic:

Crime is linked to poor education.

Such statements are rarely completely true. There is usually an exception that needs to be considered. Caution can be shown in several ways:

Crime **may** be linked to poor education.   *(modal verb)*

Crime is **frequently** linked to poor education.   *(adverb)*

Crime **tends to** be linked to poor education.   *(verb)*

■ Complete the table below with more examples of each.

Modals	Adverbs	Verb/phrase
can	commonly	tends to

▶ See Unit 2.7 Generalisations

3 Using modifiers

Another way to express caution is to use **quite**, **rather** or **fairly** before an adjective.

a **fairly** accurate summary

a **rather** inconvenient location

quite a significant discovery

NB. **quite** is often used before the article. It is generally used positively, while **rather** tends to be used negatively.

■ **Insert quite/ rather/ fairly in the following to emphasise caution.**

(a) The company's efforts to save energy were successful.

(b) The survey was a comprehensive study of student opinion.

(c) His second book had a hostile reception.

(d) The first year students were fascinated by her lectures.

(e) The latest type of arthritis drug is expensive.

4 Practice A

■ **Rewrite the following sentences in a more cautious way.**

(a) Private companies are more efficient than state-owned businesses.

(b) Exploring space is a waste of valuable resources.

(c) Older students perform better at university than younger ones.

(d) Word-of-mouth is the best kind of advertising.

(e) English pronunciation is confusing.

(f) Some cancers are caused by psychological factors.

(g) Global warming will cause the sea level to rise.

(h) Most shopping will be done on the internet in ten years' time.

5 Caution in verbs

When referring to sources, the verb used indicates the degree of caution appropriate. Compare:

> Tilic (2004) **states** that the cost of living . . .
> *(positive)*

> Lee (2007) **suggests** that more research is needed . . .
> *(cautious)*

Other verbs which imply tentative or cautious findings are:

> think/ consider/ hypothesise/ believe/ claim/ presume

▶ See Unit 3.14 Verbs of reference

6 Practice B

■ Re-write the following text in a more cautious style.

> **6.1**   A team of American scientists have found a way to
> reverse the ageing process. They fed diet
> supplements, found in health food shops, to elderly rats,
> which were then tested for memory and stamina. The animals
> displayed more active behaviour after taking the supplements,
> and their memory improved. In addition, their appearance
> became more youthful and their appetite increased. The
> researchers say that this experiment is a clear indication of
> how the problems of old age can be overcome. They state that
> in a few years' time everyone will be able to look forward to a
> long and active retirement.

Conjunctions

Conjunctions are words or phrases which join parts of a sentence together, or link a sentence to the next one. Effective reading and writing requires clarity about their meaning. This unit describes the different functions of conjunctions and practises their use. Other ways of linking sections of text are explained in Unit 2.3 Cohesion.

1 Types of conjunctions

■ **Study the way conjunctions work in the following:**

Demand for food is increasing **because** the population is growing. (reason)

Mechanisation has increased crop yields, **yet** production is still inadequate. (opposition)

■ **Underline the conjunctions in the following sentences.**

(a) A few inventions, for instance television, have had a major impact on everyday life.

(b) Furthermore, many patients were treated in clinics and surgeries.

(c) The definition of 'special needs' is important since it is the cause of some disagreement.

(d) The technology allows consumers a choice, thus increasing their sense of satisfaction.

(e) Four hundred people were interviewed for the survey, then the results were analysed.

(f) However, another body of opinion associates globalisation with unfavourable outcomes.

■ **There are six main types of conjunction. Match each of the types below to one of the sentences above.**

(i)   Addition   (**b**)

(ii) Result   (   )

(iii) Reason   (   )

(iv) Opposition   (   )

(v)   Example   (   )

(vi) Time   (   )

2 Practice A

When reading a text, conjunctions are a kind of signpost to help the reader follow the ideas.

■ **Read the paragraph below and underline the conjunctions, then decide what their functions are (i.e. types i – vi above).**

2.1   **BIOFUELS**

Newly published research examines some important questions about the growing use of biofuels, <u>such as</u> ethanol made from maize. The production of these has increased sharply recently, but the replacement of food crops with fuel crops has been heavily criticised. Although initially seen as a more environmentally-friendly type of fuel, the research shows that producing some biofuels, for instance biodiesel palm oil, is more polluting than using conventional oil. The ethanol produced from sugar cane, however, can have negative emissions, in other words taking carbon dioxide from the atmosphere instead of adding it. Consequently, it can be seen that the situation is rather confused, and that biofuels are neither a magic solution to the energy problem, nor are they the environmental disaster sometimes suggested.

Conjunction	Type	Conjunction	Type
(a) *such as*	*example*	(f)	
(b)		(g)	
(c)		(h)	
(d)		(i)	
(e)		(j)	

3 Common conjunctions

■ Complete the table with as many examples of conjunctions as possible.

Addition	Result	Reason	Opposition	Example	Time
				such as	

4 Practice B

■ Insert a suitable conjunction into each gap.

(a) _____ checking the equipment the experiment was repeated.

(b) _____ most people use the train, a minority walk or cycle.

(c) Brick is a thermally efficient building material. It is, _____, cheap.

(d) Demand has increased for summer courses, _____ extra ones are offered this year.

(e) Many writers, _____ Chekhov, have been doctors.

(f) _____ the increase in residence fees more students are moving out.

(g) _____ Mustafa was in the lecture his car was being repaired.

(h) _____ he was studying Italian he spent a semester in Bologna.

5 Practice C

■ Insert a suitable conjunction into each gap.

5.1 GEOENGINEERING

Geoengineers believe that it may be possible to counteract the effects of global warming by large scale engineering projects, (a)_____ the 'solar umbrella' designed to reflect sunlight back into space. (b)_____ no major schemes have yet been attempted, there is already controversy about the risks involved.

Two different approaches are suggested: (c)_____ to block incoming sunlight, (d)_____ alternatively to take carbon dioxide out of the atmosphere. One proposal, (e)_____, consists of putting iron into the sea in order to encourage the growth of the tiny sea creatures that absorb carbon dioxide. (f)_____ this second approach is unlikely to create major problems, blocking sunlight is potentially dangerous, (g)_____ the risk of affecting rainfall patterns (h)_____ even ocean currents. (i)_____ bioengineers are anxious to establish clear guidelines before any large-scale experiments are carried out.

6 Conjunctions of opposition

Note the position of the conjunctions in the following examples:

> The economy is strong, **but/ yet** there are frequent strikes.
>
> **Although/ while** there are frequent strikes the economy is strong.
>
> **In spite of/ despite** the frequent strikes the economy is strong.
>
> There are frequent strikes. **However/ nevertheless**, the economy is strong.

■ **Write two sentences in each case.**

Example:

The equipment was expensive/ unreliable.

(i)   The equipment was expensive but unreliable.

(ii) Although the equipment was expensive it was unreliable.

(a) The government claimed that inflation was falling. The opposition said it was rising.

(i)   _____

_____

(ii) _____

_____

(b) This department must reduce expenditure. It needs to install new computers.

(i)   _____

_____

(ii) _____

_____

(c) Sales of the new car were poor. It was heavily advertised.

(i)   _____

_____

(ii) _____

_____

7 Practice D

Finish the sentences in a suitable way.

(a) In contrast to America, where gun ownership is common,

_____

(b) Despite leaving school at the age of 14

_____

(c) The majority displayed a positive attitude to the proposal, but

_____

(d) While the tutor insisted that the essay was easy,

_____

(e) Although the spring was cold and dry

_____

Nouns and adjectives

It is easy to confuse the noun and adjective form of words such as 'possibility' and 'possible'. This unit gives examples of some of the most common pairs, and provides practice with their use. See also Unit 3.2 Academic vocabulary.

1 Using nouns and adjectives

■ **Compare these sentences:**

The **efficiency** of the machine depends on the **precision** of its construction.

Precise construction results in an **efficient** machine.

The first sentence uses the nouns 'efficiency' and 'precision'. The second uses adjectives: 'precise' and 'efficient'. Although the meaning is similar the first sentence is more formal. Effective academic writing requires accurate use of both nouns and adjectives.

2 Practice A

■ **Complete the gaps in the table below.**

Noun	Adjective	Noun	Adjective
approximation	approximate		particular
superiority		reason	
	strategic		synthetic
politics		economics/ ecomony*	
	industrial		cultural
exterior		average	
	high		reliable
heat		strength	
	confident		true
width		probability	
	necessary		long
danger		relevance	

* Compare the three nouns:

Economics is a demanding undergraduate degree course. (academic subject)

The Greek **economy** is heavily in debt. (national economy, countable)

Economy is needed to reduce the deficit. (saving money, uncountable)

3 Practice B

■ **Insert a suitable noun or adjective from the table in each sentence.**

(a) The students were _____ their project would be successful.

(b) One of Tokyo's _____ is its excellent transport system.

(c) There is a strong _____ that fees will rise next year.

(d) The students complained that the lecture was not _____ to their course.

(e) The results are so surprising it will be _____ to repeat the experiment.

(f) The _____ household size in Turkey is 4.1.

(g) Regularly backing up computer files reduces the _____ of losing vital work.

(h) Revising for exams is a tedious _____.

(i) These data appear to be _____ and should not be trusted.

(j) The _____ date of the founding of Rome is 750 BC.

(k) The _____ consequences of the war were inflation and unemployment.

(l) They attempted to make a _____ of all the different proposals.

4 Practice C

■ **Underline the adjective in each sentence and write the related noun in brackets.**

Example:

Several steel producers are <u>likely</u> to shut down next year. (*likelihood*)

(a) The HR team have just completed a strategic review of pay.

(_____)

(b) Dr Lee adopted an analytical approach to the inquiry.

(_____)

(c) Nylon was one of the earliest synthetic fibres. (_____)

(d) Her major contribution to the research was her study of ante-natal care. (_____)

(e) All advertising must respect cultural differences.

(_____)

(f) Some progress was made in the theoretical area.

(_____)

(g) A frequent complaint is that too much reading is expected.

(_____)

(h) We took a more critical approach to marketing theory.

(_____)

(i) The Department of Social Policy is offering three courses this year. (_____)

(j) Finally, the practical implications of my findings will be examined. (_____)

5 Abstract nouns

A range of nouns is used to express common ideas in academic writing:

Political geography is an interesting **field**.

The **concept** of class was first discussed in the eighteenth century.

Drucker developed a new **approach** in his second book.

■ **Read the following and find a synonym for each word in bold from the box below (there are more words than sentences).**

(a) The second **factor** in the recession was the loss of confidence.

(b) Smith's **concept** of the division of labour was first presented in 1776.

(c) Snow is a rare **phenomenon** in Rome.

(d) The President's resignation gave a new **aspect** to the national crisis.

(e) A barcode scanner is a **device** used at supermarket checkouts.

(f) Her **field** is integrating content and language learning.

(g) The World Bank is a **body** created to support developing countries.

(h) Mendel's work on genetics provided new **perspectives** for agronomists.

(i) Their main **concern** is to prevent a further increase in crime.

(j) The new **system** allows errors to be detected in 12 seconds.

(k) The survey identified three **categories** of voluntary workers.

(l) The most serious **issue** raised at the meeting was student accommodation.

process	organisation	machine	theory
event	types	worry	answer	area
views	cause	feature	problem

Prefixes and suffixes

Prefixes and suffixes are the first and last parts of certain words. Understanding the meaning of prefixes and suffixes can help you work out the meaning of a word, and is particularly useful when you meet specialist new vocabulary.

1 How prefixes and suffixes work

'Unsustainable' is an example of a word containing a prefix and suffix. Words like this are much easier to understand if you know how prefixes and suffixes affect word meaning.

Prefixes change or give the meaning.

Suffixes show the meaning or the word class (e.g. noun, verb).

Prefix	Meaning	STEM	Suffix	Word class/Meaning
un-	negative	**sustain**	**-able**	adjective/ability

The rate of growth was **unsustainable**. (*i.e. could not be continued*)

2 Prefixes

(a) Negative prefixes: UN-, IN-, MIS- and DIS- often give adjectives and verbs a negative meaning: **un**clear, **in**capable, **mis**hear, **dis**agree

(b) A wide variety of prefixes define meaning e.g. PRE- usually means 'before', hence **pre**fer, **pre**history and, of course, **pre**fix!

Common prefixes of meaning

■ Find the meaning(s) of each prefix (NB. some prefixes have more than one meaning).

Prefix	Example	Example sentence
auto	automatically	Over-18s **automatically** have the right to vote.
co	co-ordinator	The **co-ordinator** invited them to a meeting.
ex	ex-president	The **ex-president** gave a lecture on climate change.
ex	exclusive	It is difficult to join such an **exclusive** club.
macro	macroeconomics	Keynes focused on **macroeconomics**.
micro	microscope	She examined the tiny animals with a **microscope**.
multi	multinational	Ford is a **multinational** motor company.
over	oversleep	He missed the lecture as he **overslept**.
post	postpone	The meeting is **postponed** until next Monday.
re	retrain	The firm **retrained** the staff to use the new software.
sub	subtitle	Chinese films often have **subtitles** in the West.
under	undergraduate	Most **undergraduate** courses last three years.
under	undercook	Eating **undercooked** meat can be dangerous.

3 Practice A

Prefixes allow new words to be created.

■ Suggest possible meanings for the recently developed words in bold.

(a) Criminal activity seems to be very common among the **underclass**.

(b) The passengers found the plane was **overbooked** and had to wait for the next flight.

(c) The **microclimate** in this district allows early vegetables to be grown.

(d) It is claimed that computers have created a **post-industrial** economy.

(f) Most film stars have **ex-directory** phone numbers.

(g) The class was **underwhelmed** by the quality of the lecture.

4 Suffixes

(a) Some suffixes like –ION, -IVE or –LY help the reader find the word class e.g. noun, verb or adjective.

(b) Other suffixes add to meaning, e.g. –FUL or –LESS after an adjective have a positive or negative effect (thought**ful**/ care**less**).

5 Word class suffixes

Nouns	-ER often indicates a person: *teacher, gardener* -EE can show a person who is the subject: *employee, trainee* -ISM and –IST are often used with belief systems and their supporters: *socialism/ socialist* -NESS converts an adjective into a noun: *sad/ sadness* -ION changes a verb to a noun: *convert/ conversion*
Adjectives	-IVE *effective, constructive* -AL *commercial, agricultural* -IOUS *precious, serious*
Verbs	-ISE / -IZE to form verbs from adjectives: *private/ privatise* NB. In the USA only –ize spelling is used, but both forms are accepted in the UK
Adverbs	-LY most (but not all) adverbs have this suffix: *happily*

6 Meaning suffixes

A few suffixes contribute to the meaning of the word:

> -ABLE has the meaning of 'ability': a **watchable** film, **changeable** weather

> -WARDS means 'in the direction of': the ship sailed **northwards**

> -FUL and -LESS: **hopeful** news, a **leaderless** team

7 Practice B

■ **Give the word class and suggest possible meanings for:**

(a) cancellation   (f) unpredictable

(b) coincidental   (g) saleable

(c) unco-operatively   (h) interviewee

(d) evolutionary   (i) consumerism

(e) protester   (j) symbolically

8 Practice C

■ **Study each sentence and find the meaning of the words underlined.**

(a) The film is a French-Italian <u>co-production</u> made by a <u>subsidiary</u> company.

(b) When the car crashed she screamed <u>involuntarily</u> but was <u>unharmed</u>.

(c) Using <u>rechargeable</u> batteries has <u>undoubted</u> benefits for the environment.

(d) The <u>unavailability</u> of the product is due to the <u>exceptional</u> weather.

(e) There is a <u>theoretical</u> possibility of the machine <u>disintegrating</u>.

▶ See Unit 3.2 Academic vocabulary

3.8 Prepositions

Prepositions are generally short words such as 'by' or 'at' which are often linked to nouns, verbs and adjectives. Their use may seem confusing, but this unit explains how they can be understood. Students should consult a standard English grammar for a full list of prepositional combinations.

1 Using prepositions

■ Underline the prepositions in the following text (ignoring to + infinitives).

1.1 The purpose of this paper is to examine the development of the textile industry in Catalonia over the period 1780–1880. This clearly contributed to the region's industrialisation, and was valuable for stimulating exports. In conclusion, the paper sets out to demonstrate the relationship between the decline in agricultural employment and the supply of cheap labour in the factory context.

■ The table lists the main ways of using prepositions. Find one example of each in the text 1.1.

Noun + preposition	*purpose of*
Verb + preposition	
Adjective + preposition	
Phrasal verb	
Preposition of place	
Preposition of time	
Phrase	

Note the difference between phrasal verbs and verbs with prepositions:

> The cars are **made in** Korea. (verb + preposition = easy to understand)

> The researcher **made up** some of his data. (phrasal verb = hard to understand)

2 Practice A

■ Study these further examples of preposition use and decide on their type.

(a) There are a number **of** limitations to be considered . . .
      (*noun +*)

(b) The results would be applicable **to** all children . . .
      (_____)

(c) . . . the data was gathered **from** a questionnaire.
      (_____)

(d) All the items were placed **within** their categories.
      (_____)

(e) The results **of** the investigation are still pertinent . . .
(_____)

(f) The respondents had spent **on** average 4.9 years . . .
(_____)

(g) . . . most countries **in** sub-Saharan Africa . . .
(_____)

(h) . . . **within** a short spell of four years.
(_____)

3 Prepositions and nouns

■ **Insert a suitable preposition before or after the nouns in the sentences below.**

(a) Evidence is presented in support _____ the value of women's work.

(b) A small change _____ wind direction can lead to large temperature changes.

(c) Many examples _____ tax evasion were found.

(d) The answer _____ the problem was 0.585.

(e) Globalisation, _____ a political sense, involves a loss of national authority.

(f) The second point is their impact _____ developing countries.

4 Prepositions in phrases

■ **Complete the following phrases with the correct preposition.**

(a) _____ the whole   (e) in support _____

(b) point _____ view   (f) _____ the other hand

(c) in respect _____   (g) _____ order to

(d) _____ spite of   (h) standard _____ living

5 Prepositions of place and time

Note the difference between 'among' and 'between':

> **Among** 14 students in the class, only two were from Africa. *(large group)*
>
> He divided his time **between** the offices in Barcelona and Madrid. *(limited number)*

■ **Complete the following sentences with suitable prepositions of place or time.**

(a) _____ the respondents, few had any experience of working abroad.

(b) The illiteracy rate declined gradually _____ 1976 _____ 1985.

(c) Most workers _____ the European Union retire before the age _____ 60.

(d) Leonardo da Vinci was born _____ Florence _____ 1452.

(e) Chocolate sales fall _____ summer and peak _____ Christmas.

(f) _____ the surface, there is no difference _____ male and female responses.

6 Practice B

■ **Complete the following text with suitable prepositions.**

This study sets (a)_____ to answer the controversial question (b)_____ whether increased food supply (c)_____ a country makes a significant contribution (d)_____ reducing malnutrition (e)_____ children. It uses data collected (f)_____ 75 countries (g) _____ 1969 and 1987. The findings are that there was a considerable improvement (h)_____ the majority (i)_____ countries, despite increases in population

(j)_____ the period. However, a clear distinction
was found (k)_____ the poorest countries (e.g.
(l)_____ South Asia), where the improvement was
greatest, and the wealthier states such as those
(m)_____ North Africa. Other factors, notably the
educational level (n)_____ women, were also found to
be critical (o)_____ improving childhood nutrition.

Punctuation

> Accurate punctuation and use of capitals help the reader to understand exactly what the writer meant. While some aspects of punctuation, such as the use of commas, can be a matter of individual style, correct punctuation in areas such as quotation is important.

1 Capitals

It is difficult to give precise rules about the use of capital letters in modern English. However, they should be used in the following cases:

(a) The first word in a sentence   *In the beginning . . .*

(b) Names of organisations   *Sheffield Hallam University*

(c) Days and months   *Friday 21 July*

(d) Nationality words   *France and the French*

(e) Names of people/ places   *Dr Martin Lee from Sydney*

(f) Book titles (main words only)   *Power and the State*

2 Apostrophes (')

These are one of the most misused features of English punctuation. They are mainly used in two situations:

(a) to show contractions

He's the leading authority

(NB. contractions are not common in academic English)

(b) with possessives

The professor's secretary *(singular)*

Students' marks *(plural)*

3 Semi-colons (;)

They are used to show the link between two connected phrases, when a comma would be too weak and a full stop too strong.

20 people were interviewed for the first study; 33 for the second.

Semi-colons are also used to divide up items in a list when they have a complex structure, as in a multiple citation:

(Maitland, 2006; Rosenor, 1997; New Scientist, 2006b; University of Michigan, 2000).

NB. semi-colons are quite rare in many types of writing.

4 Colons (:)

(a) to introduce explanations

The meeting was postponed: the Dean was ill.

(b) to start a list

Three aspects were identified: financial, social and . . .

(c) to introduce a quotation

As the Duchess of Windsor said: 'You can never be too rich or too thin'.

5 Commas

There is some flexibility in the use of commas, and overuse can slow down the reader. Some examples of necessary comma usage are:

> However, more cases should be considered before reaching a conclusion.
>
> Certain crops, for instance wheat, are susceptible to diseases.
>
> Three hundred people were interviewed, but only half the responses could be used.

6 Quotations marks/ inverted commas (" "/' ')

(a) Single quotation marks are used to emphasise a word:

> The word 'factory' was first used in the seventeenth century.

to give quotations from other writers:

> Goodwin's (1977) analysis of habit indicates that, in general, 'it will be more difficult to reverse a trend than to accentuate it'.

to show direct speech:

> 'Can anyone find the answer?' asked the lecturer.

NB. Longer quotations are usually indented (i.e. have a wider margin) and/ or are set in smaller type.

(American English uses double quotation marks to show quotations).

(b) Double quotation marks are used to show quotations inside quotations (nested quotations):

> As Kauffman remarked: 'his concept of "internal space" requires close analysis.'

(c) In references, quotation marks are used for the names of articles and chapters, but book or journal titles normally use italics:

> Russell, T. (1995) 'A future for coffee?' *Journal of Applied Marketing* 6, 14–17.

▶ **See Unit 1.8 References and quotations**

7 Others

Hyphens (–) are used with certain words and structures:

well-engineered/ co-operative/ three-year-old

Exclamation marks (!) and question marks (?)

'Well!' he shouted, 'Who would believe it?'

Brackets or parentheses ( ) can be used to give additional detail:

Relatively few people (10–15 per cent) were literate in
sixteenth-century Russia.

8 Practice A

■ **Punctuate the following sentences.**

(a) the study was carried out by christine zhen-wei qiang of the
national university of singapore

(b) professor rowans new book the end of privacy is published in
new york

(c) as keynes said its better to be roughly right than precisely
wrong

(d) three departments law business and economics have had their
funding cut

(e) as cammack 1994 points out latin america is creating a new
phenomenon democracy without citizens

(f) thousands of new words such as app enter the english
language each year

(g) the bbcs world service is broadcast in 33 languages including
somali and vietnamese

(h) she scored 56 per cent on the main course the previous
semester she had achieved 67 per cent

9 Practice B

■ Punctuate the following text.

9.1   the school of biomedical sciences at borchester university is offering two undergraduate degree courses in neuroscience this year students can study either neuroscience with pharmacology or neuroscience with biochemistry there is also a masters course which runs for four years and involves a period of study abroad during november and december professor andreas fischer is course leader for neuroscience and enquiries should be sent to him via the website

Singular or plural?

The choice of singular or plural can be confusing in various situations, such as in the use of countable and uncountable nouns. This unit illustrates the main areas of difficulty and provides practice with these.

1 Five areas of difficulty

The main problem areas for international students are shown below.

(a) Nouns should agree with verbs, and pronouns with nouns:

Those problems are unique.

There are many arguments in favour.

(b) Uncountable nouns and irregular plurals usually have no final 's':

Most students receive free **tuition**.

The main export is tropical **fruit**.

(c) General statements normally use the plural:

State **universities** have lower **fees**.

(d) 'Each/ every' are followed by singular noun and verb forms:

Every **student gets** financial support.

(e) Two linked nouns should agree:

Both the **similarities** and **differences** are important.

■ **Find the mistake in each of the following sentences and decide what type (a – e above) it is.**

(a) The proposal has both advantages and disadvantage.
    (_____)

(b) A majority of children in Thailand is vaccinated against measles. (_____)

(c) There are few young people in rural area.
    (_____)

(d) Many places are experiencing an increase in crimes.
    (_____)

(e) Each companies have their own policies.
    (_____)

2 Group phrases

■ **Study the following 'group' phrases.**

singular + plural	plural + singular	plural + uncountable
half the universities a range of businesses one of the elements	two types of institution various kinds of course many varieties of response	three areas of enquiry several fields of research rates of progress

Note that if a verb has more than one subject it must be plural, even if the preceding noun is singular:

Scores of students, some teachers and the president **are** at the meeting.

Their valuable suggestions and hard work **were** vital.

Certain 'group' nouns, e.g. team/ army/ government can be followed by either a singular or plural verb:

The team **was** defeated three times last month. *(collectively)*

The team **were** travelling by train and bus. *(separately)*

3 Uncountable nouns

(a) Most nouns in English are countable, but the following are generally uncountable, i.e. they are not usually used with numbers or the plural 's'.

accommodation	information	scenery
advice	knowledge	staff
behaviour	money	traffic
commerce	news	travel
data	permission	trouble
education	progress	vocabulary
equipment	research	weather
furniture	rubbish	work

Many of these can be 'counted' by using an extra noun:

A piece of advice.

Three patterns of behaviour.

An item of equipment.

Six members of staff.

(b) Another group of uncountable nouns is used for materials:

wood/ rubber/ iron/ coffee/ paper/ water/ oil/ stone

Little **wood** is used in the construction of motor vehicles.

Huge amounts of **paper** are needed to produce these magazines.

Many of these nouns can be used as countable nouns with a rather different meaning:

Over 20 daily **papers** are published in Delhi.

Most **woods** are home to a wide variety of birds.

(c) The most difficult group can be used either as countable or uncountable nouns, often with quite different meanings (further examples: business/ capital/ experience):

She developed **an interest** in genetics. *(countable)*

The bank is paying 4 per cent **interest**. *(uncountable)*

Other nouns with a similar pattern are used for general concepts (love/ fear/ hope):

Most people feel that **life** is too short *(in general)*

Nearly 20 **lives** were lost in the mining accident *(in particular)*

4 Practice A

■ **In the following sentences, choose the correct alternative.**

(a) Little/ few news about the accident was released.

(b) He established three successful businesses/ business in 2008.

(c) Substantial experiences/ experience of report writing are/ is required.

(d) It is often claimed that travel broadens/ travels broaden the mind.

(e) Paper was/ papers were very expensive in the twelfth century.

(f) How much advice/ many advices were they given before coming to Australia?

(g) She had little interest/ few interests outside her work.

(h) The insurance policy excludes the effects of civil war/ wars.

(i) Irons were/ iron was first powered by electricity in the twentieth century.

(j) They studied the work/ works of three groups of employees over two years.

5 Practice B

■ **Read the text and choose the correct alternative.**

> **5.1**   A large number of <u>company/ companies</u> <u>has/ have</u> developed <u>website/ websites</u> in the last few years. Trading using the internet is called <u>e-commerce/ e-commerces</u>, and <u>this/ these</u> <u>is/ are</u> divided into two main kinds: B2B and B2C. The former involves trading between <u>business/ businesses</u>, but many <u>company/ companies</u> want to use the internet to sell directly to <u>its/ their</u> customers (B2C). However, large numbers have experienced <u>trouble/ troubles</u> with <u>security/ securities</u> and other practical issues. In addition, the high start-up costs and the <u>expense/ expenses</u> of advertising <u>means/ mean</u> that <u>this/ these</u> <u>company/ companies</u> often struggle to make a profit.

Synonyms

Synonyms are different words with a similar meaning. A good
writer uses them to avoid repetition and thus provide more
interest for the reader. Synonyms should also be used when
paraphrasing or note-making to avoid plagiarism.

1 How synonyms work

■ Underline the synonyms in the following text and complete the table.

1.1   Royal Dutch Shell is the **largest** oil company in the world by revenue, with
a significant share of the global hydrocarbon market. The **giant** firm
employs over 100,000 people internationally, including over 8,000 employees in
Britain.

word/phrase	synonym
largest	*giant*
oil	
company	
in the world	
people	

(a) Synonyms are not always exactly the same in meaning, but it is important not to change the register. 'Firm' is a good synonym for 'company', but 'boss' is too informal to use for 'manager'.

(b) Many common words e.g. culture, economy or industry have no effective synonyms.

2 Common synonyms in academic writing

■ Match the academic synonyms in each list.

Nouns		Verbs	
area	advantage	accelerate	change
authority	part	achieve	help
behaviour	argument	alter	question
beliefs	disadvantage	analyse	suggest
benefit	tendency	assist	explain
category	**field**	attach	evolve
component	source	challenge	examine
concept	emotion	claim	establish
controversy	target	clarify	insist
drawback	explanation	concentrate on	speed up
expansion	conduct	confine	take apart
feeling	topic	develop	join
framework	possibility	eliminate	reach
goal	ethics	evaluate	decrease
hypothesis	production	found	demonstrate
interpretation	research	maintain	increase
issue	theory	predict	cite
method	increase	prohibit	reinforce
option	idea	quote	remove
quotation	citation	raise	focus on
results	figures	reduce	forecast
statistics	type	respond	ban
study	structure	retain	limit
trend	system	show	keep
output	findings	strengthen	reply

▶ See Unit 3.2 Academic vocabulary

3 Practice A

■ **Find synonyms for the words and phrases underlined, re-writing the sentence where necessary.**

(a) Professor Hicks <u>questioned</u> the <u>findings</u> of the <u>research</u>.

_____

(b) The <u>statistics</u> <u>show</u> a steady <u>expansion</u> in applications.

_____

(c) The institute's <u>prediction</u> has caused a major <u>controversy</u>.

_____

(d) Cost seems to be the <u>leading</u> <u>drawback</u> to that <u>system</u>.

_____

(e) They will <u>concentrate on</u> the first <u>option</u>.

_____

(f) After the lecture she tried to <u>clarify</u> her <u>concept</u>.

_____

(g) Three <u>issues</u> need to be <u>examined</u>.

_____

(h) The <u>framework</u> can be <u>retained</u> but the <u>goal</u> needs to be <u>altered</u>.

_____

(i) OPEC, the oil producers' cartel, is to <u>cut production</u> to <u>raise</u> global prices.

_____

(j) The <u>trend</u> to smaller families has <u>speeded up</u> in the last decade.

_____

4 Practice B

■ **Identify the synonyms in this text by underlining them and linking them to the word they are substituting for.**

Example: agency – organisation

4.1   The chairman of the UK's food standards **agency** has said that a national advertising campaign is necessary to raise low levels of personal hygiene. The **organisation** is planning a £3m publicity programme to improve British eating habits. A survey has shown that half the population do not wash before eating, and one in five fail to wash before preparing food. There are over six million cases of food poisoning in this country every year, and the advertising blitz aims to cut this by 20 per cent. This reduction, the food body believes, could be achieved by regular hand washing prior to meals.

5 Practice C

■ **In the following text, replace all the words or phrases in bold type with suitable synonyms.**

5.1   Many motor manufacturers are currently planning to start making electric cars. Their **plan** is to **make cars** that are cheaper and less polluting. But the **motor manufacturers** face several key difficulties. One **key difficulty** is the limited range of the battery, while another **difficulty** is its cost and weight. But the **motor manufacturers** predict that these **difficulties** will soon be overcome and **predict** that 10 per cent of cars will be powered by electricity in five years' time.

3.12 Time words

Time words such as 'during' and 'since' are often used in introductions or general statements. The use of some of these words is restricted to particular tenses. See also Unit 3.15 Verbs – tenses.

1 How time words are used

■ **Study the use of the following:**

She went on a training course **for** six weeks.	(with numbers, without start date)
The report must be finished **by** 12 June.	(on or before)
He has been president **since** 2007.	(with present perfect, must specify start date)
They are studying in Bristol **until** March.	(end of a period)
The library was opened two years **ago.**	(usually with past)
The hotel is closed **during** the winter.	(with nouns)

Before writing he studied over 100 sources.	(often followed by –ing form; also **after)**
He applied in May and was accepted two months **later.**	(often used with numbers; also **earlier)**

2 Time words and tenses

■ Compare the tenses used with the following time words and phrases:

Last year there **was** an election in Spain.	(past)
In the last year there **has been** a decline in inflation.	(present perfect)
Recently, there **has been** a sharp rise in internet use.	(present perfect)
Currently, there **is** widespread concern about plagiarism.	(present)

3 Practice A

■ Choose the best alternative in each case.

(a) Currently/ recently she has been researching the life cycle of a Brazilian wasp.

(b) He worked there until/ during he retired.

(c) Dr Hoffman has lived in Melbourne since/ for sixteen years.

(d) Last month/ in the last month a new book was published on capital punishment.

(e) Applications must be received by/ on 25 November.

(f) Since/ during her arrival last May she has reorganised the department.

(g) During/ for the winter most farmers in the region find work in the towns.

4 Practice B

■ Study the schedule for Professor Wang's recent trip and complete the sentences below with a suitable word. It is now 16 April.

March 12	Fly London – Barcelona
March 13–14	Conference in Barcelona
March 15	Train Barcelona – Paris
March 16	Lecture visit to Sorbonne
March 17	Fly Paris – Shanghai
March 18–19	Meeting with colleagues
March 20	Fly Shanghai – London

(a) _____ month Professor Wang made a lengthy trip.

(b) _____ her trip she visited three countries.

(c) _____ 18 March she had travelled 11,000 kilometres.

(d) She was away from home _____ nine days altogether.

(e) A month _____ she was in Paris.

(f) Two days _____ she was in Shanghai.

(g) She stayed in Shanghai _____ 20 March.

(h) _____ she is writing a report on her trip.

5 Practice C

■ Complete each gap in the following text with a suitable word.

| **5.1** | **EATING OUT** |

(a)_____ the last few decades there has been a
significant change in eating habits in the UK.
(b)_____ the early 1980s eating out in restaurants
and cafes has increased steadily. There are several reasons for
this trend.

50 years (c)_____ most women were housewives,
and cooked for their families every day. But
(d)_____, with more women working outside the
home, less time has been available for food preparation.
(e)_____, 71 per cent of women aged 20–45 are at
work, and (f)_____ 2020 it is estimated that this
will rise to 85 per cent.

Another factor is the growth in disposable income, which has
risen significantly (g)_____ the late 1970s. With
more money in their pockets people are more likely to save
the trouble of shopping and cooking by visiting their local
restaurant.

---

6 Practice D

■ Study the details of Napoleon's life, and complete the biography below
(one word per gap).

1769   Born in Corsica

1784   Entered military school in Paris

1789   French revolution started

1793   Promoted to brigadier general

1796   Appointed to command army of Italy; married Josephine

1799   Returned from Egypt and became First Consul of France

1807   France controlled most of continental Europe

1810   Divorced Josephine and married Marie-Louise, daughter of Austrian emperor

1812   Forced to retreat from Russia

1814   Exiled to island of Elba

1815   Defeated at battle of Waterloo and exiled to island of St Helena

1821   Died in exile

6.1   NAPOLEON

Napoleon entered military school at the age of 15, five years (a)_____ the start of the French revolution. He quickly gained promotion, becoming brigadier general at 24 and commander of the Italian army three years (b)_____. At the age of 30 he was effectively the French dictator, and due to his military genius France controlled most of Europe (c)_____ 1807. When he divorced his first wife, Josephine, in 1810, they had been married (d)_____ 14 years. (e)_____ the divorce he married Marie-Louise, an Austrian princess. His campaigns were successful (f)_____ 1812, but in that year the disastrous retreat from Moscow marked the start of his decline. However, (g)_____ his years of absolute power he had made significant changes to European law and government. Although he died nearly 200 years (h)_____, Napoleon's influence is still felt throughout the European continent.

Verbs – passives

The passive form is a feature of much academic writing, making it more impersonal and formal, but the passive should not be used exclusively. This unit provides practice in developing a balanced style.

1 Active and passive

The passive is used when the writer wants to focus on the result, not on the cause:

The college was founded in 1925 by Walter Trimble. *(passive)*

Walter Trimble founded the college in 1925. *(active)*

In the first sentence, the emphasis is on the college, in the second on Trimble. So the passive is often used in written English when the cause (a person or thing) is less important or unknown.

Aluminium **was** first **produced** in the nineteenth century. *(by someone)*

The colony **was abandoned** in the 1630s. *(due to something)*

The cause of the action can be shown by adding 'by . . .':

> The city was flooded **by a severe hurricane**.

The passive is also used in written work to provide a more impersonal style:

> The findings **were evaluated**. *(not 'I evaluated the findings')*

▶ **See Unit 2.10 Style**

2 Structure

All passive structures have two parts:

Form of the verb to be	Past participle
is	constructed
was	developed
will be	re-organised

■ **Change the following into the passive.**

(a) We collected the data and compared the two groups.

(b) I interviewed 120 people in three social classes.

(c) They checked the results and found several errors.

(d) We will make an analysis of the findings.

(e) He asked four doctors to give their opinions.

(f) She wrote the report and distributed ten copies.

3 Using adverbs

An adverb can be inserted in a passive form to add information:

> This process is **commonly** called 'networking'.

■ Change the following sentences from active to passive and insert a suitable adverb from the box below (more words than sentences). Decide if it is necessary to show a cause.

Example:

The recession forced half the companies to go out of business.

Half the companies were **eventually** forced to go out of business by the recession.

(a) The Connors family ran the company until 1981.

(b) Dr Weber has predicted that prisons will be unnecessary in the future.

(c) They provided pencils for all students in the exam.

(d) The researchers calculated the percentages to three decimal places.

(e) The students handed in the essays on Tuesday morning.

(f) She researched the life cycle of over 15 types of mice.

optimistically	helpfully	punctually	accurately
eventually	vividly	carefully	profitably

4 Practice A

In most texts the active and the passive are mixed.

■ **Read the following text and underline the passive forms.**

4.1   BOOTS

When John Boot died at 45, he was worn out by the effort of establishing his herbal medicine business. He had spent his early years as a farm labourer but had worked his way up to be the owner of a substantial business. He was born in 1815, became a member of a Methodist chapel in Nottingham, and later moved to the city. John was concerned by the situation of the poor, who could not afford a

continued . . .

cont.	doctor, and in 1849 he opened a herbal medicine shop which was called the British and American Botanic Establishment. In the early stages John was helped financially by his father-in-law, while his mother provided herbal knowledge.

On his death in 1860 the business was taken over by his wife, and she was soon assisted by their 10-year-old son, Jesse. He quickly showed the business ability which transformed his father's shop into a national business. Jesse opened more shops in poor districts of the city and pioneered advertising methods. He also insisted on doing business in cash, rather than offering his customers credit.

5 Practice B

■ List the passives in the table below. Decide if the active could be used instead, and re-write it if so.

Passive	Active possible?	Active
He was worn out	Yes	The effort … had worn him out

■ **What would be the effect of using the passive throughout the text?**

6 Practice C

The passive is used more in written than in spoken English, but should not be overused, as it can give a very formal tone.

■ **In the following text, which continues the history of the Boots company, passives are used throughout. Change some of them into the active.**

6.1 In 1889 he was introduced to Florence Rowe, the daughter of a bookseller, while on holiday. After they were married the business was affected by her ideas: the product range was enlarged to include stationery and books. The Boots subscription library and in-store cafes were also introduced due to Florence's influence. During the first world war the Boots factories were used to make a variety of products, from sterilisers to gas masks. But after the war Jesse was attacked by arthritis and, worried by the economic prospects, the company was sold to an American rival for £2m. This, however, was made bankrupt during the Depression and Boots was then bought by a British group for £6m, and Jesse's son, John, was made chairman. The famous No.7 cosmetics range was launched in the 1930s and in the second world war both saccharin and penicillin were produced in the factories. However, recently the company has been threatened by intense competition from supermarkets in its core pharmaceutical business.

3.14 Verbs of reference

When introducing quotations or summaries of other writers'
ideas it is necessary to use verbs of reference such as 'claims' or
'states'. These verbs indicate the position of the writer whose
ideas are being summarised. This unit gives examples of
common verbs of reference and practises their use. See also
Unit 1.8 References and quotations.

1 Using verbs of reference

Referring verbs are used to summarise another writer's ideas:

> Previn **argued** that global warming was mainly caused by the
> solar cycle.

> Bakewell (1992) **found** that most managers tended to use
> traditional terms . . .

They may also be used to introduce a quotation.

> . . . as Scott **observed:** 'Comment is free but facts are sacred'.

2 Common referring verbs

Most of these verbs are followed by a noun clause beginning with 'that'.

(a) The following mean that the writer is presenting a case:

> argue   claim   consider   hypothesise   suggest
>   believe   think   state

> Melville (1997) **suggested** that eating raw eggs could be harmful.

(b) A second group describe a reaction to a previously stated position:

> accept   admit   agree   deny   doubt

> Handlesmith **doubts** Melville's suggestion that eating raw eggs . . .

(c) Others include:

> assume   conclude   discover   explain   imply
>   indicate   maintain   presume   reveal   show

> Patel (2003) **assumes** that inflation will remain low.

3 Practice A

▪ Write a sentence referring to what the following writers said (more than one verb may be suitable). Use the past tense.

Example:
Z: 'My research shows that biofuels are environmentally neutral'.

Z **claimed/ argued** that biofuels were environmentally neutral.

(a) A: 'I may have made a mistake in my calculations on energy loss'.

_____

_____

(b) B: 'I did not say that women make better doctors than men'.

_____

_____

(c) C: 'Small firms are more dynamic than large ones'.

_____

_____

(d) D: 'I support C's views on small firms'.

_____

_____

(e) E: 'I'm not sure, but most people probably work to earn money'.

_____

_____

(f) F: 'After much research, I've found that allergies are becoming more common'.

_____

_____

(g) G: 'I think it unlikely that electric cars will replace conventional ones'.

_____

_____

(h) H: 'Somebody should investigate the reasons for the increase in winter storms'.

_____

_____

(i) I: 'There may be a link between crime and sunspot activity'.

_____

_____

4 Further referring verbs

A small group of verbs is followed by the pattern

(somebody/ thing + for + noun/ gerund):

> Lee (1998) **blamed** the media for creating uncertainty.

>   blame   censure   commend   condemn   criticise

NB. All except 'commend' have a negative meaning.

Another group is followed by

(somebody/ thing + as + noun/ gerund):

> Terry **interprets** rising oil prices as a result of the Asian recovery.

>   assess   characterise   classify   define   describe
>   evaluate   identify   interpret   portray   present

5 Practice B

Rewrite the following statements using verbs from the lists in (4).

Example:

K: 'Guttman's work is responsible for many of the current social problems.'

K **blamed** Guttman's work for many of the current social problems.

(a) L: 'She was very careless about her research methods'.

_____

(b) M: 'There are four main types of children in care'.

_____

(c) N: 'That company has an excellent record for workplace safety'.

_____

(d) O: 'The noises whales make must be expressions of happiness'.

_____

(e) P: 'Wind power and biomass will be the leading green energy sources'.

_____

(f) Q: 'Darwin was the most influential naturalist of the nineteenth century'.

_____

(g) R: 'An insect is a six-legged arthropod'.

_____

(h) S: 'Law students are hard-working but open-minded'.

_____

Verbs – tenses

This unit focuses on the main tenses used in academic writing and explains the way their use is controlled by time words, which were examined in Unit 3.12.

1 Using tenses

■ **Decide which tenses are used in the following examples (verbs in bold) and complete the table overleaf to explain why.**

(a) According to Hoffman (1996) small firms **respond** more rapidly to change . . .

(b) Currently, student numbers **are falling** but class sizes **are rising**.

(c) Since the summer house prices **have increased** steadily.

(d) In the last three years more students **have been working** part-time.

(e) Two years ago the island **opened** its third airport.

(f) During the winter **she was studying** Japanese history.

(g) The report was published in June. It showed that in 2009 profits **had increased** by 55 per cent.

(h) The forecast concludes that infection rates **will peak** next month.

	Tense	Reason for use
a	*Present simple*	*General rule*
b		
c		
d		
e		
f		
g		
h		

2 Practice A

■ **Complete the following sentences by using the most suitable tense for the verb in brackets.**

(a) Home ownership _____ (rise) steadily since 1950.

(b) DIY _____ (stand for) do it yourself.

(c) Last year they _____ (sell) nearly five million books.

(d) By the time he died in 1987 he _____
(take out) over 50 patents.

(e) In ten years most people in the world
_____ (have) a mobile phone.

(f) At the moment the class _____ (work) on
an engineering project.

(g) The professor _____ (give) a lecture
when the earthquake happened.

(h) Lee (1965) _____ (dispute) Sakamoto's
theory.

(i) In the last six years inflation _____ (fall)
sharply in Europe.

3 Simple or continuous?

(a) In general, the continuous is used to focus on the activity itself or to
stress its temporary nature. Compare the following:

She **has been writing** that report for six days.
(to show duration of temporary activity)

He **is writing** an article on probability theory.
(to show temporary nature of activity)

She **writes** stories for teenage girls.
(to demonstrate her normal work)

(b) Also note that certain verbs are rarely used in the continuous. They
are **state** verbs such as prefer, own and believe. Another similar group
is known as **performative** verbs (assume, deny, promise, refuse,
suggest).

■ **Select either simple or continuous in each case:**

(a) This year the team at Yale _____ (work)
on a study of rice farming in Indonesia.

(b) He _____ (believe) he will finish the book
early next year.

(c) This magazine _____ (look for) a writer
on business law.

(d) Two years ago she was managing a branch but now she
_____ (run) the head office.

(e) The average age of marriage in Italy
_____ (rise) by six years between 1970
and 1990.

(f) The company _____ (own) factories in
12 countries.

(g) Most people in the city _____ (live)
within two kilometres of their work.

(h) Dr McPherson _____ (attend) a
conference in South America this week.

4 Using time phrases

When writing paragraphs, it is important to be clear about which time
phrases control the tenses of verbs.

■ **Study the following paragraph:**

4.1   **THE AMERICAN FAMILY**

<u>Recently</u>, the condition of the family **has produced** some of the
strongest debate heard in America. The statistics of collapse
have appeared simple and clear. The proportion of children
born outside marriage **rose** from 18 per cent in <u>1980</u> to 33 per
cent in <u>1999</u>. The share of households made up of two parents
and their children **fell** from 45 per cent in <u>1960</u> to only 23 per
cent in <u>2000</u>.

The time phrase *Recently* controls the tense of the first two sentences
(present perfect). The next two sentences are in the simple past because
of the dates *1980, 1999, 1960* and *2000*, which show finished periods:

Time phrase	Verbs controlled
Recently	has produced
	have appeared
1980	rose
1999	fell
1960	
2000	

5 Practice B

◼ Read the text below and select the most suitable tense for each verb in brackets, considering the time phrases in bold.

5.1 THE BOLOGNA PROCESS

The first university in Europe was founded in Bologna, Italy, in 1088. **In 1999,** 911 years later, European education ministers (a)_____ (meet) there to plan a common framework for universities in Europe. The aim (b)_____ (be) to standardise the system of studying for degrees to permit students to study in different countries. After 11 years of preparation, **in 2010**, a meeting of 46 ministers in Leuven, Belgium, (c)_____ (agree) the creation of a European higher education area. This (d)_____ (allow) students to take the credits they have gained in one country and transfer them to a degree programme in another.

It seems that many governments **currently** (e)_____ (support) the process as a method of reforming their universities, which (f)_____ (face) strong competition from America. The international league tables continue to be dominated by the 'Ivy League' universities, which (g)_____ (have) much higher incomes than most European institutions. The USA (h)_____ (spend) twice as much of its GDP on higher education as the European average. But **in future** the Bologna process (i)_____ (give) universities more freedom to employ and promote staff, which (j)_____ (make) them more competitive with their transatlantic counterparts. **By 2020** it is hoped that universities in Europe (k)_____ (be) better funded and more independent.

Writing models

Formal letters and emails

Although less common than before electronic communication became available, letters are still important for formal matters, or when an email address is unknown. They are also considered to be more reliable than emails.

However, due to its convenience email is increasingly used for semi-formal as well as informal communication. It is widely seen as a way of having a permanent record of an arrangement or discussion.

1 Letters

You have applied for a place on an MSc course at a British university. Read the letter on p. 250 you have received in reply.

■ **Label the following features of formal letters with the letters (a-l) from the left margin.**

(d) Date	( ) Address of recipient	
( ) Ending	( ) Address of sender	
( ) Request for response	( ) Reason for writing	
( ) Greeting	( ) Sender's reference	
( ) Further details	( ) Signature	
( ) Subject headline	( ) Writer's name and job title	

(a)   Central Admissions Office
                                                            Wye House
                                                            Park Campus
                                                      University of Mercia
                                                      Borchester BR3 5HT
                                                        United Kingdom

(b) Ms P Tan
       54 Sydney Road
       Rowborough RB1 6FD

(c) Ref: MB/373

(d) 3 May 2010

(e) Dear Ms Tan,

(f) **Application for MSc Sustainable Building Technology**

(g) Further to your recent application, I would like to invite you to the university for an informal interview on Tuesday 21st May at 11 am. You will be able to meet the course supervisor, Dr Schmidt, and look round the School of the Built Environment.

(h) A map of the campus and instructions for finding the university are enclosed.

(i) Please let me know if you will be able to attend on the date given.

(j) Yours sincerely,

(k) *M. Bramble*

(l) Mick Bramble
       Administrative Assistant
       Central Admissions Office

Enc.

Note the following points:

(a) The example above is addressed to a known individual and the ending is 'Yours sincerely'. However, when writing to somebody whose name you do not know, e.g. The Manager, use *Dear Sir* and *Yours faithfully*.

(b) A formal letter generally uses the family name in the greeting (*Dear Ms Tan*). Certain organisations may, however, use a first name with a family name or even a first name alone (*Dear Jane Tan, Dear Jane*).

(c) If the sender includes a reference it is helpful to quote it in your reply.

2 Practice A

■ **Write a reply to Mr Bramble making the following points:**

(a) You will attend the interview on the date given.

(b) You would like to have the interview one hour later, due to train times.

---

54 Sydney Road
Rowborough RB1 6FD

3 Emails

Starting and finishing

The following forms are acceptable ways to begin an email if you know the recipient:

> Hi Sophie, Dear Sophie, Hello Sophie

If you have not met the recipient it may be safer to use:

> Dear Sophie Gratton, Dear Ms Gratton, Dear Dr Gratton

If you need to send an email to a large group (e.g. colleagues) you may use:

> Hi everyone, Hello all

In all cases to close the message you can use:

> Regards, Best wishes, Best regards

You may also add a standard formula before this:

> Look forward to meeting next week/ Let me know if you need further information.

The main text

Here you can use common contractions (I've, don't) and idiomatic language, but the normal rules for punctuation should be followed to avoid confusion. Spelling mistakes are just as likely to cause misunderstanding in emails as elsewhere. Always check for spelling and grammar problems before pressing the 'send' key. Note that emails tend to be short, although longer documents may be added as attachments.

4 Practice B

■ **Read the following and decide who the sender and recipient might be. Would Rachel expect a reply?**

Hello Dr Hoffman,

I'm afraid I can't attend your Accounting Methods class this week, as I have to go for a job interview then. However, I will be there next Tuesday, when I am giving my paper (attached, as requested).

See you then,

Rachel

---

5 Practice C

■ **Write suitable emails for the following situations:**

(a) You are writing to Mark, a colleague at work, to ask him to suggest a time to meet you tomorrow.

(b) Write to your teacher, Tricia James, to ask her to recommend another book for your current essay.

(c) Write to a group of classmates asking them how they want to celebrate the end of the course.

(d) Write an email in response to the one below. You have never had this book.

According to our records, the copy of *Special Needs in Education* you borrowed from the library on 12 October is now overdue. Your fine is currently £2.15. Please arrange to return this book as soon as possible.

Best wishes,

Tim Carey
Library services

Writing CVs

A CV (US resumé) is a summary of your education and work experience used when applying for a job. This unit illustrates the most common format and explains the main points to consider when preparing or updating your own.

1 The contents of a CV

A CV is a personal statement over which you have complete control. When you apply for a job your CV will probably be one of dozens seen by the firm's HR department, so in order to impress it should be as clear, accurate and well-presented as possible. Even if the writers are highly qualified, CVs that contain irrelevant material, are badly organised and include spelling mistakes may well cause the sender to be rejected.

Note the following:

- There is no need to give your gender, date of birth or marital status.

- Two sides is the maximum that most employers want to read.

- Details should be relevant to the particular job you are applying for.

- Avoid clichéd claims such as 'team worker' or 'self starter'.

- Information such as education details is normally presented in reverse chronological order (i.e. the most recent comes first).

- Details of your early education or hobbies are probably irrelevant to the post.

2 Practice A

■ Study the example CV below. How could it be improved?

Charles Moreno
31 Cavendish Avenue
London SW3 5GT
07356–723837
cmoreno@swiftserve.net

PROFILE
I am a recent marketing graduate with a background in psychology and some valuable experience of running mixed-media campaigns, looking for a rewarding position that will allow me to build on my knowledge and qualifications.

EDUCATION

Oct 2009–Sep 2010	Mercia Business School, Borchester
	MSc Marketing (modules included Marketing Studies; Operational Marketing; Marketing Contexts)
Sep 2005–Jun 2008	West London University, London
	BSc Psychology (2.1) (Research project in group behaviour)
Sep 2003–Jun 2005	Trent Valley College, Newark
	A-Levels in Psychology, English and German

EMPLOYMENT

Aug 2008–Jul 2009	Voluntary post with 'Help the Homeless' organising fund-raising campaign. Experience with designing leaflets and posters, contacting press and preparing viral marketing strategy.
Jan 2006–May 2007	Part-time post as office assistant with Advantage Market Research, Holland Park, London. General office duties and interviewing.

SKILLS and QUALIFICATIONS
- fluent German speaker
- familiar with most common software, e.g. Excel, MS Office
- clean driving licence

3 Practice B

■ Write a CV for yourself. When you are satisfied with the format, store it electronically so it can be updated when necessary.

Reports, case studies and literature reviews

Although essays are the most common assignments in many academic disciplines, students of science and business are often asked to write reports. Both essays and reports may include sections looking at one example in detail (case studies) or evaluating other published research on the topic (literature reviews). This unit examines the organisation of these types of text and provides examples.

1 Writing reports

While essays are often concerned with abstract or theoretical subjects, a report is a description of a situation or something that has happened. In academic terms it might describe:

(a) an experiment you have conducted

(b) a survey you have carried out

(c) a comparison of alternative proposals to deal with a situation

Clearly there is a big difference between describing a scientific laboratory experiment and reporting on students' political opinions. In some areas, e.g. laboratory work, your teachers will make it clear what format you should follow. However, most reports should include the following features:

Introduction
- background to the subject
- reasons for carrying out the work
- review of other research in the area

Methods
- how you did your research
- description of the tools/ materials used

Results
- what you discovered
- comments on likely accuracy of results

Discussion
- of your main findings
- comments on the effectiveness of your research

Conclusion
- summary of your work
- suggestions for further research

2 Essays and reports

In comparison with essays, reports are likely to

(a) be based on primary as well as secondary research

(b) use numbering (1.1, 1.2) and sub-headings for different sections

(c) be more specific and detailed

In most other respects, reports are similar to essays, since both:

(a) have a clear and logical format

(b) use objective and accurate academic style

(c) include citations and references

(d) make use of visual information in the form of graphs and tables

(e) include appendices where necessary

■ **Decide whether the following topics are more likely to be written as reports or essays.**

Topic	Report	Essay
1 The development of trade unions in South Africa		
2 Two alternative plans for improving the sports centre		
3 A study you conducted to compare male and female attitudes to eating		
4 An overview of recent research on the human genome		
5 The arguments for and against capital punishment		

▶ **For an example of report writing see Unit 4.4 Designing and reporting surveys**

3 Case studies

A case study is a detailed example. It may be the main subject of an essay, or part of a longer report. In either case it is intended to show exactly what happened in a particular situation. For example, if you are discussing methods of fighting malaria in rural areas, a case study might follow the real-life efforts of a medical team in a specific district of Indonesia over a period of months.

What are the advantages of including case studies?

_____

_____

_____

What are the disadvantages?

_____

_____

_____

■ Match the topics on the left with the case studies on the right.

Topics	Case studies
Methods of teaching dyslexic children Improving crop yields in semi-deserts Reducing infant mortality Building earthquake-resistant bridges Dealing with re-offending among prisoners Improving recycling rates in large cities	A programme to cut smoking among pregnant women in a Greek clinic Work and learning – how a Brazilian scheme encouraged convicts to stay out of jail The Berlin experiment: increasing public participation in collecting and sorting waste Using solar power to operate irrigation pumps in Ethiopia The lessons from Chile – how three structures withstood the 2010 quake An experimental approach to reading difficulties with under-8s in Singapore

4 Example case study

■ Read the following example and answer the questions below.

Topic: *Adapting international brands to local markets*

Case study: *The experience of IKEA in China*

4.1 Introduction

The Chinese economy has expanded at an annual rate of over 8 per cent for the past 30 years. Parallel to this, the Chinese furniture industry has grown vigorously, with annual sales recently rising by over 20 per cent a year. Legislation to privatise home ownership and rapidly rising income levels have created unprecedented growth in the home improvement market. According to estimates from the Credit Suisse group, China will be the world's second largest furniture market by 2014. This demand has boosted domestic production and also prompted international furniture manufacturers to enter this lucrative market.

IKEA, a Swedish furniture company, was one of the international companies to move into China. It is a major furniture retailer operating in over 40 countries around the world and has annual sales of over 21 billion euros (IKEA website). It entered the Chinese market in 1998 with its first store in Beijing, and sees great potential in the country, having already expanded to ten stores and five distribution centres. Despite this successful growth, IKEA has found itself facing a number of challenges in terms of local differences in culture and business practices.

Marketing IKEA in China

Marketing management needs to be largely tailored to local contexts. IKEA has kept this notion in mind when designing marketing strategies and trying to appeal to local customers while maintaining profitability. The company attempts to find the best possible compromise between standardisation and adaptation to the local markets. Its product policy pays careful attention to Chinese style and integrates the set of product attributes effectively (Armstrong and Kotler, 2006).

The store layouts reflect the floor plan of many Chinese apartments, and since many of these have balconies, the stores include a balcony section. In contrast with traditional Chinese furniture, which is dark with much carving, IKEA introduces a lighter and simpler style. However, efforts have been made to adapt its products to Chinese taste. For instance, it has released a series of products just before each Chinese New Year. In 2008, the year of the rat, the series 'Fabler' was designed, using the colour red, which is associated with good luck.

Changes were also made to some product ranges. In Sweden, people are used to sleeping in single beds, or to putting two single beds together to form a double bed.

continued . . .

cont. However, this idea was not very well received by Chinese couples, due to the fact that sleeping in separate beds symbolises a poor relationship and is believed to bring bad luck. In addition, Chinese brand names should have positive connotations. The Chinese name of IKEA (Yi Jia) means 'comfortable home', which gives the company a useful advantage in the market.

An important feature of a retailer is the services it offers. The Shanghai store, for instance, has a children's playground and a large restaurant, which make it distinctive. However, Chinese consumers expect free delivery and installation, and although IKEA has reduced its charges for these, it still compares unfavourably with its competitors.

Price

When the company first entered China its target market was couples with an income of 5–8,000 Rmb per month. Following steady price reductions this has now been lowered to families with just over 3,000 Rmb. Various strategies have been adopted to achieve these reductions; the most effective being to source locally. 70 per cent of its products sold in China are now made in the country (Song, 2005). Furthermore, IKEA replaced its thick, annual catalogue with thinner brochures which now appear five times a year. These not only cut printing costs but also give greater flexibility to adjust prices.

Accessibility is also an important issue for the Chinese market. In most countries IKEA stores are sited near main roads, but as only 20 per cent of likely customers own cars in China, easy access to public transport is vital (Miller, 2004).

Advertising plays an important role in the total promotional mix. IKEA uses advertising effectively, with adverts in the local newspapers to keep customers informed of special offers. All TV commercials are produced locally with Chinese characters. Public relations is also vital to building a good corporate image. In China, IKEA co-operates with the Worldwide Fund for Nature (WWF) on forest projects. The company insists on using environmentally friendly and recyclable materials for the packaging of their products, as part of their efforts to build a good corporate image.

Discussion and conclusion

IKEA's product policy in China has been to successfully standardise products as much as possible, but also customise as much as needed. But it has learned that

continued . . .

cont. service is also vital: free delivery and installation are the perceived rules in the local market which it needs to follow. It has further found that it is better to locate in a downtown area, easily accessible with public transport, when free delivery is not provided.

International companies which operate in China, such as IKEA, face more complicated marketing decisions than local companies. They must become culture-conscious and thoroughly research local requirements rather than simply introduce a standard model of business.

(a) What has IKEA done to adapt to the Chinese market?

_____

_____

_____

_____

(b) Give examples of problems the company has faced in this market.

_____

_____

_____

_____

(c) What could be done to improve the case study?

_____

_____

_____

_____

5 Literature reviews

In most papers a summary of relevant and recent authorities on the subject is included in the introduction. Only a minority have a separate section headed 'The Literature' or 'Literature Review', although this is standard in dissertations. In all cases it is usually necessary to show that you are familiar with the main sources, so that your writing can build on these. Occasionally the whole focus of an essay may be a lengthy literature review, but in most student writing it will only form a relatively short section of the paper.

A literature review is not simply a list of sources that you have studied. It can be used to show that there is a gap in the research that your work attempts to fill:

> This article has a different standpoint from other studies, because it believes that the influence of the state on the market has structurally increased since the neo-liberal era.

> This article focuses on information production, not information accessibility. That is the difference between this research and previous studies . . .

It is also common to use the literature section to clarify the varying positions held by other researchers:

> The political competition literature comprises two main strands – voter monitoring and political survival.

Writers may also show how changes in thought have appeared at different times:

> Of late, a number of papers (Besley *et al.*, 2006; Besley and Preston, 2007; Persson and Tabellini, 2000) have collated the various arguments . . .

▶ See Unit 1.9 Combining sources

6 Example literature review

■ Study the following example, from a student essay on motivation theory. Answer the questions which follow.

6.1 CONTENT AND PROCESS THEORIES

The various theories of motivation are usually divided into content theories and process theories. The former attempt to 'develop an understanding of fundamental human needs' (Cooper *et al.,* 1992: 20). Among the most significant are Maslow's hierarchy of needs theory, McClellan's achievement theory and Herzberg's two-factor theory. The process theories deal with the actual methods of motivating workers, and include the work of Vroom, Locke and Adams.

Content theories

Maslow's hierarchy of needs theory was first published in 1943 and envisages a pyramid of needs on five levels, each of which has to be satisfied before moving up to the next level. The first level is physiological needs such as food and drink, followed by security, love, esteem and self-fulfillment (Rollinson, 2005: 195–6). This theory was later revised by Alderfer, who reduced the needs to three: existence, relatedness and growth, and re-named it the ERG theory. In addition, he suggested that all three needs should be addressed simultaneously (Steers *et al.,* 2004: 381). McClelland had a slightly different emphasis when he argued that individuals were primarily motivated by three principal needs: for achievement, affiliation and power (Mullins, 2006: 199).

In contrast, Herzberg suggested, on the basis of multiple interviews with engineers and accountants during the 1950s, a two-factor theory: that job satisfaction and dissatisfaction had differing roots. He claimed that so-called hygiene factors such as conditions and pay were likely to cause negative attitudes if inadequate, while positive attitudes came from the nature of the job itself. In other words, workers were satisfied if they found their work intrinsically interesting, but would not be motivated to work harder merely by good salaries or holiday allowances. Instead workers needed to be given more responsibility, more authority or more challenging tasks to perform (Vroom and Deci, 1992: 252). Herzberg's work has probably been the most influential of all the theories in this field, and is still widely used today, despite being the subject of some criticism, which will be considered later.

Process theories

Vroom's expectancy theory hypothesises a link between effort, performance and motivation. It is based on the idea that an employee believes that increased effort

continued . . .

cont.   will result in improved performance. This requires a belief that the
individual will be supported by the organisation in terms of training and
resources (Mullins, 2006). In contrast, Locke emphasised the importance of setting
clear targets to improve worker performance in his goal theory. Setting
challenging but realistic goals is necessary for increasing employee motivation:
'goal specificity, goal difficulty and goal commitment each served to enhance task
performance' (Steers *et al.*, 2004: 382). This theory has implications for the design
and conduct of staff appraisal systems and for management by objective methods
focusing on the achievement of agreed performance targets.

Another approach was developed by Adams in his theory of equity, based on the
concept that people value fairness. He argued that employees appreciate being
treated in a transparently equitable manner in comparison with other workers
doing similar functions, and respond positively if this is made apparent (Mullins,
2006). This approach takes a wider view of the workplace situation than some
other theories, and stresses the balance each worker calculates between 'inputs'
i.e. the effort made, and 'outputs', which are the rewards obtained.

(a) How many types of motivation theory are described?

_____

_____

(b) How many different theorists are mentioned?

_____

_____

(c) How many sources are cited?

_____

_____

(d) Why has the writer not referred to the work of the theorists
directly but used secondary sources instead?

_____

_____

@ Reports, Case studies and Literature reviews>

Designing and reporting surveys

Surveys, in which people are asked questions about their
behaviour or opinions, are a common feature of academic work.
This unit deals with the design of effective questionnaires for
surveys, and presents a suitable structure for reporting the
results.

1 Conducting surveys

■ **What are the reasons for carrying out surveys? List your ideas below.**

(a) *To replicate other research* _____

_____

(b) _____

_____

(c) _____

_____

(d) _____

_____

2 Questionnaire design

(a) Which is the better question?

    (i) How old are you?

    (ii) Are you (a) under 20 (b) between 21 – 30 (c) over 30?

(b) What is the main difference between the two questions below?

    (i) What do you think of university students?

    (ii) Do you think university students are (a) lazy (b) hardworking (c) average

(c) How many questions should your questionnaire contain?

When designing your questionnaire:

(a) Limit the number of questions so the respondent can answer them in a minute or two. Long and complicated questionnaires will not receive accurate replies.

(b) Keep questions clear and simple, and not too personal.

(c) Closed questions (bii) are easier to process, but open questions (bi) will collect a wider range of responses.

(d) You should try putting the questions to a classmate before beginning the full survey, and be ready to modify any that were not clear.

3 Survey language

■ Study the report of a survey carried out on a university campus. Complete the report by inserting suitable words from the box below into the gaps (more words than gaps).

sample	conducted	method	respondents	random	questions
majority	questioned	mentioned	interviewees	common	
questionnaire	unusual	generally	minority	slightly	

3.1 STUDENT EXPERIENCE OF PART-TIME WORK

Introduction

With the introduction of course fees and the related increase in student debt, more students are finding it necessary to work part-time. The survey was (a)_____ to find out how this work affects student life and study.

Method

The research was done by asking students selected at (b) _____ on the campus to complete a (c) _____ (see Appendix 1). 50 students were (d) _____ on Saturday 23 April, with approximately equal numbers of male and female students.

Table 1 Do you have or have you had a part-time job?

	Men	**Women**	**Total**	**%**
Have job now	8	7	15	30
Had job before	4	6	10	20
Never had job	14	11	25	50

Findings

Of the (e) _____ , 30 per cent currently had part-time jobs, 20 per cent had had part-time jobs, but half had never done any work during university semesters (see Table 1). (f) _____ who were working or who had worked were next asked about their reasons for taking the jobs. The most common reason was lack of money (56 per cent), but many students said that they found the

continued . . .

cont.   work useful experience (32 per cent) and others
(g) _____ social benefits (12 per cent).

The 25 students with work experience were next asked
about the effects of the work on their studies. A significant
(h) _____ (64 per cent) claimed that there were
no negative effects at all. However, 24 per cent said that their
academic work suffered (i) _____ , while a small
(j) _____ (12 per cent) reported serious adverse
results, such as tiredness in lectures and falling marks.

Further (k) _____ examined the nature of the
work that the students did. The variety of jobs was surprising,
from van driver to busker, but the most (l) _____
areas were catering and bar work (44 per cent) and secretarial
work (32 per cent). Most students worked between 10 and 15
hours per week, though two (8 per cent) worked over 25
hours. Rates of pay were (m) _____ near the
national minimum wage, and averaged £6.20 per hour.

The final question invited students to comment on their
experience of part-time work. Many (44 per cent) made the
point that students should be given larger grants so that they
could concentrate on their studies full-time, but others felt
that they gained something from the experience, such as
meeting new people and getting insights into various work
environments. One student said that she had met her current
boyfriend while working in a city centre restaurant.

Conclusions

It is clear that part-time work is now a common aspect of
student life. Many students find jobs at some point in their
studies, but an overwhelming majority (88 per cent) of those
deny that it has a damaging effect on their studies. Most
students work for only 2–3 hours per day on average, and a
significant number claim some positive results from their
employment. Obviously, our survey was limited to a relatively
small (n) _____ by time constraints, and a fuller
study might modify our findings in various ways.

4 Question forms

Question 1 is given above Table 1. What were the other questions in this survey?

■ **Using the report, write possible questions below.**

2 _____

_____

3 _____

_____

4 _____

_____

5 _____

_____

6 _____

_____

7 _____

_____

5 Tenses

What is the main tense in (a) Findings (b) Conclusion?

■ **Explain the reasons for the difference.**

_____

_____

_____

_____

_____

6 Practice

■ You are preparing a survey on one of the following subjects.
Write a questionnaire of no more than six questions to collect the most
useful data.

(a) Patterns of student spending

(b) Student satisfaction with teaching methods

(c) Customer attitudes to taxi companies

Writing longer essays

> Long essays of 2,500–5,000 words may be required as part of a module assessment. These require more research and organisation than short essays, and this unit provides a guide to how such an assignment may be tackled.

1 Planning your work

Longer assignments are normally set many weeks before their deadline, which means that students should have plenty of time to organise their writing. However, it is worth remembering that at the end of a semester you may have to complete several writing tasks, so it may be a good idea to finish one earlier.

You should also check the submission requirements of your department. These include style of referencing, method of submission (i.e. electronic, hard copy or both) and place and time of submission. Being clear about these will avoid last-minute panic.

(a) The first thing is to prepare a schedule for your work. An eight-week schedule might look like the example on p. 274.

(b) How you actually plan your schedule is up to you, but the important thing is to organise your time effectively. Leaving the writing stage until the last minute will not lead to a good mark, however much research you have done. Although you may be tempted to postpone writing, the sooner you start the sooner you will be able to begin refining your ideas. Remember that late submission of coursework is usually penalised.

Week	Stages of work	Relevant units in Academic Writing
1	Study title and make first outline. Look for and evaluate suitable sources.	1.4
2	Reading and note-making. Keep record of all sources used.	1.2A, 1.2B, 1.5, 1.8
3	Reading, note-making, paraphrasing and summarising. Modify outline.	1.2A, 1.2B, 1.5, 1.7, 1.8
4	Write draft of main body.	1.10
5	Write draft introduction and conclusion.	1.11
6	Re-write introduction, main body and conclusion, checking for logical development of ideas and relevance to title.	1.12
7	Organise list of references, contents, list of figures and appendices if required. Check all in-text citations.	1.8, 3.14
8	Proofread the whole essay before handing it in. Make sure that the overall presentation is clear and accurate.	1.12

(c) Longer papers may include the following features, in this order:

Title page	Apart from the title, this usually shows the student's name and module title and number.
Contents page	This should show the reader the basic organisation of the essay, with page numbers.
List of tables or figures	If the essay includes visual features such as graphs, these need to be listed by title and page number.
Introduction	
Main body	If a numbering system is used, the chief sections of the main body are normally numbered 1, 2, 3 and then subdivided 1.1, 1.2 etc.
Conclusion	
List of references	This is a complete list of all the sources cited in the text. Writers occasionally also include a bibliography, which is a list of sources read but not cited.
Appendices (Singular – appendix)	These sections are for data related to the topic, which the reader may want to refer to. Each appendix should have a title and be mentioned in the main body.

2 Example essay

■ **Read the following essay on the topic of nuclear energy. In pairs or groups, discuss the following points:**

(a) What is the writer's position on this issue?

(b) How does the writer make his/her position clear?

2.1 EVALUATE THE RISKS OF USING NUCLEAR ENERGY AS AN ALTERNATIVE TO FOSSIL FUELS

Introduction

The search for sources of energy began when humans first started to burn wood or other forms of biomass to generate heat for cooking and smelting. This was followed by using hydropower from rivers and harnessing wind energy with windmills. Later the exploitation of chemical energy began with the burning of coal, oil and natural gas. Then, in the middle of the twentieth century, nuclear energy appeared for the first time, with the hope that it would allow the efficient production of cheap, clean energy (Bodansky, 2004).

Nuclear energy has, however, become the subject of considerable debate, with its proponents claiming that it is beneficial for the environment, since its production does not create carbon dioxide (CO_2) which can lead to global warming. However, its opponents argue that it can damage the environment by creating radioactive waste. It is also linked to diseases in humans, and there is the additional fear that it may be abused by terrorists in future. These critics further argue that other energy sources, such as solar power, could constitute safer alternatives to fossil fuels without posing an environmental threat.

This essay attempts to assess the risks of using nuclear power, in comparison with other sources of energy. The main arguments for employing nuclear energy are first considered, followed by an examination of the safety issues around this source of power, including the safety and security concerns connected with nuclear waste.

1 Reasons for using nuclear energy

1.1 An alternative source of energy

The rationale behind using nuclear energy stems from the need to find alternative energy sources to fossil fuels, i.e. oil, gas and coal, which are finite. This is a growing concern, due to the increase in the global population, which is accompanied by an increase in energy demand. Mathew (2006) indicates that the annual energy consumption rate per capita in developed countries is between 4,000 and 9,000 kgs of oil, while the rate in less developed countries is around 500 kgs. As a result, the demand for total primary energy, which will accompany

continued . . .

cont.   the population growth, is projected to increase from 12.1 Mtoe (million
tons of oil equivalent) to 16.1 Mtoe in 2030. If this increase occurs the total
global stock of oil and gas would only be adequate for 250 years, thus requiring
the urgent development of other energy sources, which would not deplete the
stock of natural resources available for future generations.

1.2 Limitations of other energy sources

Wind energy and solar power are frequently presented as alternative energy
sources to fossil fuels. Both are freely available in many parts of the world and
their use involves no CO_2 emissions. Sterrett (1994) claims that sufficient wind
energy exists to displace approximately eight billion barrels of oil. However, wind
energy is unreliable, as wind turbines do not function if the wind speed is too high
or low. Similarly, solar power is only effective during the day, and is uneconomic
in cool and cloudy climates. Neither of these sources currently offers an efficient
and reliable alternative to energy created from fossil fuels.

1.3 Reducing carbon dioxide emissions

An important reason for using nuclear energy is to reduce the emissions of CO_2,
which are produced by burning fossil fuels. Bodansky (2004) points out that this
type of fuel is the main source of the increase in atmospheric carbon dioxide. The
amount of CO_2 produced by each source differs due to the differences in their
hydrogen content. For example, natural gas contains one carbon atom and four
hydrogen atoms, which combine with oxygen to produce CO_2. The proportion of
CO_2 is lower than with the other sources, because the emission depends on the
mass of carbon inside the chemical compounds. Although natural gas is thus
cleaner than the alternatives, burning all three fuels contributes to the greenhouse
effect, which is causing the earth to heat up.

Nuclear energy, however, emits no carbon dioxide, sulphur dioxide (SO_2) or
nitrous oxide (NOx). It is estimated that in 2003, in the USA, nuclear energy
prevented the release of 680 million tons of CO_2, 3.4 millions tons of SO_2 and
1.3 million tons of NOx. If released from coal burning plants, these gases would
have caused the deaths of 40,000 people annually (Olah *et al.*, 2006: 127).
According to Richard (2008: 273) the use of nuclear energy in France between
1980 and 1987 reduced CO_2 emissions by 34 per cent.

continued . . .

cont.   **1.4 Cost efficiency**

Nuclear energy could potentially generate more electricity than other current sources. As Murray (2000: 73) explains, a typical reactor, which consumes 4 kg/day of uranium U235, generates 3,000 MW of energy a day, while other sources such as natural gas, coal or oil require many times the equivalent of that amount of uranium to generate the same energy. Therefore nuclear energy is relatively cost efficient as it uses a cheap raw material.

In recent years the price of oil and natural gas has risen sharply, and this trend seems likely to continue in future. Lillington (2004) suggests that the cost of purchasing fuel for nuclear energy is likely to remain low compared to other energy sources, so it seems likely that this cost advantage will become a significant factor in the comparison between nuclear and other energy sources.

2 Health and safety concerns

2.1 The impact of radiation on the human body

Especially since the Chernobyl accident in 1986 there has been persistent concern about the dangers to human health from nuclear power and nuclear waste. However, it must be understood that nuclear energy is not the only source of radiation, and that there are natural sources in the environment that may be more significant. According to Bodansky (2004: 74) there is far more exposure to radiation from natural sources such as radon and cosmic rays than from all human sources, for example X-rays and nuclear medicine.

Some researchers argue that radon is one of the main causes of cancer diseases among uranium miners. However, radon may be found in all types of soil that contain uranium and radium. Bodansky (2004) points out that the concentration of radon in the soil depends on the type of soil. Hence people's exposure to radon depends on their surroundings, so that people living in houses made from limestone or wood are exposed to less radon than those living in houses built with granite. So it seems that it is not only uranium miners who are exposed to radiation, but also people in certain geological districts.

According to US law the maximum permissible exposure for those living close to nuclear plants is 1/200 rem. However, according to Hoyle (1979) this amount is just 1/20th of the radiation that can be experienced from natural background radiation.

continued . . .

cont.   It has been estimated that nuclear energy is responsible for just 20 deaths per year worldwide, although these figures are disputed by anti-nuclear campaigners who claim that the true figure is as high as 600 deaths. Hoyle (*ibid.*) claims that the average American's life-span is reduced by 1.2 hours as a result of nuclear accidents, and contrasts that with the risk from smoking, which is a loss of eight years if one packet a day is smoked. Consequently, it can be seen that the risk to human health from the use of nuclear power is extremely low.

With regard to medical treatment, which is the next largest source of exposure to radiation, X-rays will expose a patient to radiation amounts from 0.4 to 1 rad (radiation absorbed dose). A broken wrist, for instance, is likely to require 4 X-rays with a total exposure of up to 4 rads. The unit of measurement for radiation exposure is the rem, and one rem is equal to the damage caused by one rad of X-rays; the maximum amount allowed for workers in nuclear plants is five rem per year: the same as the quantity received in the course of a routine medical check-up.

2.2 The impact of radioactive waste on the environment

Nuclear energy is not alone in producing dangerous waste. Lillington (2004) estimates that nuclear energy, in the course of producing 1000 megawatts (MWe) of electricity produces annually about 30 tons of highly radioactive waste and about 800 tons of intermediate and low-level waste. In contrast, a coal-burning plant producing the same quantity of electricity would generate about 320,000 tons of coal ash, of which nearly 400 tons would be hazardous waste such as mercury and vanadium, and at least 44,000 tons of sulphur dioxide. So it can be seen that nuclear energy only produces a fraction of the dangerous wastes emitted from coal-fired power stations, and in addition does not produce greenhouse gases.

2.3 Risks of terrorism

There has been widespread concern that terrorists might steal plutonium to produce nuclear weapons. In general nuclear facilities are tightly controlled, and in practice, it would be very difficult for terrorists to use such stolen material effectively. There are alternative materials such as toxic gas that could produce equally lethal terrorist weapons. However, these concerns could be solved by

continued . . .

cont.   keeping U233 mixed with U238, which would prevent terrorist groups extracting the plutonium and fabricating a bomb.

Conclusion

The risks of nuclear energy in terms of both human health and the environment have been the subject of widespread debate and controversy. This essay has attempted to examine these risks both in terms of human health and environmental damage. It appears that many of these concerns are exaggerated, and that nuclear energy can be seen as a safe, reliable and cost effective alternative to using fossil fuels.

While all energy sources have drawbacks, nuclear should be viewed as a useful and relatively safe component in a mix of sources that can include renewables such as hydro and wind energy and non-renewables such as natural gas. The steady depletion of reserves of oil and the subsequent rise in prices is liable to emphasise this position. Clearly more could be done to make nuclear plants safer and more efficient in future, but until their value is recognised and more work is done on their design and construction their full potential is unlikely to be realised.

References

Bodansky, D. (2004) *Nuclear Energy: Principles, Practices and Prospects*. New York: Springer.

Hoyle, F. (1979) *Energy or Extinction?* London: Heinemann.

Lillington, J.N. (2004) *The Future of Nuclear Power*. Oxford: Elsevier.

Mathew, S. (2006) *Wind Energy: Fundamentals, Resource Analysis and Economics*. Berlin: Springer.

Murray, L.R. (2009) *Nuclear Energy. An Introduction to the Concepts, System and Application of the Nuclear Process*. Oxford: Butterworth.

Olah, A.G., Goeppert, A., Parakash, S. (2006) *Beyond Oil and Gas: The Methanol Economy*. Wienheim: Wiley.

Sterrett, T. (1994) *The Energy Dilemma*. London: Multivox.

3 Revision

■ Look back at the text and find examples of the following features:

(a) Background information

(b) A purpose statement

(c) An outline

(d) A definition

(e) A generalisation

(f) The use of brackets to give extra detail

(g) A passive structure

(h) A phrase showing cause and effect

(i) A synonym for 'energy'

(j) An example of tentative or cautious language

(k) An example to support the writer's argument

(l) A counter-argument

(m) A citation

(n) A synopsis

NB. Formatting of written assignments

Some departments may expect essays to be written in the style illustrated above, with numbered sections and headings, while others may require essays to be written without these. It is important to check with your teachers what the preferred style is.

Self-assessment exercises

These exercises are included to allow students to assess their progress in academic writing. The first, Describing a process, is a test of accuracy, the second, Summarising a report, tests summary writing, while the third, Problems and solutions, tests the ability to write a problem-solution paragraph.

1 Describing a process: writing an essay

■ Study the flow chart opposite, which explains the process of writing an essay. Then complete the description of the process by adding one word to each gap in the text below.

The first (a) _____ of essay writing is to read and

understand (b) _____ title, and then to prepare a

schedule of work (c) _____ the available time.

(d) _____ the topic should be brainstormed

(e) _____ a draft outline prepared. Next, possible

sources have to be evaluated (f) _____ and the

most relevant selected, after (g) _____ you can

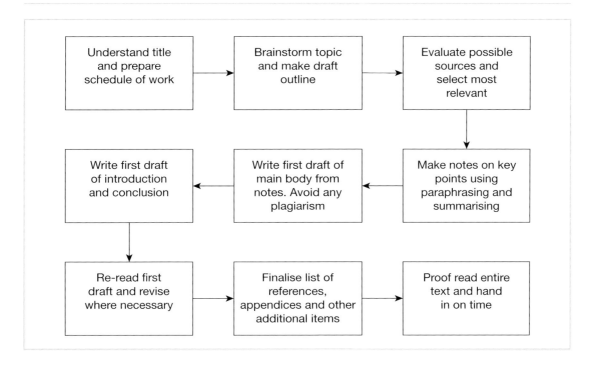

start making notes, using paraphrasing and summarising

(h) _____. When you have collected enough

material to (i) _____ the question the first draft of

the main body can (j) _____ written from the notes,

(k) _____ care to avoid any plagiarism.

Subsequently (l) _____ can write the first draft of

the introduction and conclusion, (m) _____ that a

logical approach to the title is developed. (n) _____

this the whole draft must be critically re-read and revised for

(o) _____ clarity and accuracy. The penultimate

stage is (p) _____ prepare a final list of references,

appendices and other items such as (q) _____.

Finally the whole text (r) _____ be thoroughly

proofread before handing in the assignment on time.

2 Summarising a report

■ Read the following report and write a summary in about 80 words, using the grid below (one word per space).

2.1   **CLEVER CROWS**

A group of scientists working at Oxford University have been researching the behaviour of crows. Their work, recently reported in the journal *Science*, shows that the birds appear to be able to make simple tools, a skill which was thought to be unique to man and other primates.

In the experiment a piece of meat was placed in a glass tube that was too long for the crow to reach with its beak. The bird was given a length of garden wire, nine cms long and 0.8 mm thick, to extract the meat, but it soon discovered that this was not possible if the wire was straight. The bird then held one end of the wire with its feet while it used its beak to bend the other end, making a kind of hook. This could then be used for pulling the meat out of the tube, which in most cases was done within two minutes.

It has been known for some time that chimpanzees use simple tools like sticks to reach food, but it was never thought that crows could show similar levels of intelligence. Eight years ago, however, biologists in the forests of New Caledonia watched crows using sticks to reach insects inside trees. The Oxford experiment was designed to see if the same kind of bird could modify this ability to make a tool out of a material not found in their native forests, i.e. wire.

According to Professor Kacelnik, one of the scientists involved, the research demonstrates that crows have an understanding of the physical properties of materials and the ability to adapt them for their own uses.

▶ **See Unit 1.7 Summarising**

3 Problems and solutions

You have to discuss the issue of whether it is better to assess students by course work or examination.

■ Study the points below, showing the advantages and drawbacks of each alternative. Then combine them into one paragraph using the framework given, providing your own conclusion.

	Advantages	Disadvantages
A Coursework	• all student work during semester is assessed • encourages students to work consistently during the course • students have some choice of topics	• work can be plagiarised • requires time-management skills • more difficult for teachers to assess all work fairly
B Examinations	• all students compete on equal terms • encourages students to revise all their work • reduces risk of plagiarism	• some students become nervous • only limited number of topics are assessed • time limits are unfair to non-native speakers

Problem	
Benefits of A	
Drawbacks of A	
Benefits of B	
Drawbacks of B	
Conclusion	

▶ See Unit 2.9 Problems and solutions

Glossary of terms used to discuss academic writing

Abbreviation
The short form of a word or phrase (See 3.1)

Abstract
A short summary of the aims and scope of a journal article (see 1.2B)

Acknowledgements
A list of people the author wishes to thank for their assistance, found in books and articles

Appendix
(plural – appendices) A section at the end of a book or article which contains supplementary information

Assignment
A task given to students, normally for assessment

Authority
A well-known expert on a subject

Back issue
A previous issue of a journal or magazine

Bias
A subjective preference for one point of view

Bibliography
A list of sources an author has read but not specifically cited

Brainstorm
A process of collecting ideas on a topic at random (see 1.4)

Case study
A section of an essay that examines one example in detail (see 4.3)

Citation
An in-text reference providing a link to the source (see 1.3 and 1.8)

Cohesion

Linking ideas in a text together by use of reference words (See 2.3)

Conclusion

The final section of an essay or report (see 1.11)

Contraction

A shortened form of pronoun and verb e.g. she's, I'd

Coursework

Assessed assignments given to students to complete during a course

Criteria (singular – criterion)

The principles on which something is judged or based

Deadline

The final date for completing a piece of work

Draft

The first attempt at a piece of writing

Edited book

A book with contributions from a number of writers, controlled by an editor

Extract

A piece of text taken from a longer work

Formality

In written work, the use of a non-idiomatic style and vocabulary

Format

The standard pattern of layout for a text

Heading

The title of a section of text

Higher degree

A Master's degree or Doctorate

Hypothesis

A theory that a researcher is attempting to explore/ test

Introduction

The first part of an essay or article (see 1.11)

Journal

An academic publication in a specialised area, usually published quarterly (see 1.2A)

Literature review
A section of an article describing other research on the topic in question (see 4.3)

Main body
The principal part of an essay, after the introduction and before the conclusion

Margin
The strip of white space on a page around the text

Module
Most academic courses are divided into modules, which examine a specified topic

Outline
A preparatory plan for a piece of writing (see 1.4)

Paraphrase
A re-writing of a text with substantially different wording and organisation but similar ideas

Peer-review
The process of collecting comment from academic authorities on an article before publication in a journal. This system gives increased validity to the publication.

Phrase
A few words that are commonly combined (see 1.1)

Plagiarism
Using another writer's work without acknowledgement in an acceptable manner (see 1.3)

Primary research
Original research, e.g. a laboratory experiment or a sociological enquiry

Quotation
Use of the exact words of another writer to illustrate your writing (see 1.8)

Redundancy
The unnecessary repetition of ideas or information (See 2.10)

References
A list of all the sources you have cited in your work (see 1.8)

Register
The level of formality in language

Restatement
Repeating a point in order to explain it more clearly

Scan
A method of reading in which the eyes move quickly over the page to find a specific item

Skim
A related reading technique to quickly find out the main ideas of a text

Source
The original text you have used to obtain an idea or piece of information

Summary
A shorter version of something (see 1.7)

Synonym
A word or phrase with a similar meaning to another (see 3.11)

Synopsis
A summary of an article or book

Term
Word or phrase used to express a special concept

Word class
A grammatical category, e.g. noun, adjective

Index

British Civilization
7th Edition
John Oakland

Reviews of the previous editions:

'John Oakland is the doyen of civilization studies.' – *British Studies Now*

'This is a first rate, lucidly written text.' – *G.E.C. Paton, Aston University*

The seventh edition of this highly-praised textbook has been substantially updated and revised to provide students of British studies with the perfect introduction to Britain, its country and people, politics and government, education, economy, media, arts and religion. It includes:

- discussion of recent developments and areas of topical interest in British society such as immigration, the recession, devolution and Britain's relationships with the US and the EU, and coverage of the 2010 election
- new full colour illustrations
- exercises and questions to stimulate class discussion
- updated suggestions for further reading and useful websites
- a fully updated companion website featuring further exercises, links to relevant articles and videos online, and quiz questions.

British Civilization is a vital introduction to the crucial and complex identities of Britain.

December 2010: 246x174: 360pp
Hb: 978-0-415-58327-5
Pb: 978-0-415-58328-2